Mc
TH.
DOG BEHAV

"Lynn Hoover makes a point   ...rst pages of this
unique and insightful book and   ...ne reason that this
topic is so very crucial to Animal Behavior Consultants: 'We
are not family counselors, but the truth is, to help their
dogs, families have to change too.' How true, and yet often
overlooked!"

"Hoover addresses many other "touchy" subjects. Take the
following statement: "My job is not to advance my own
agenda but to bring about the best among possible outcomes
for dogs and owners." If only all of us were willing to be this
effective! True compassion for all concerned comes from an
impartial therapeutic attitude so all parties involved feel
'safe' to express and learn. This means better information
for you, the consultant, and this attitude promotes the good
of the pet. The judgmental tendencies that many have
makes their work less effective—therefore fewer animals are
helped."

"The insight gained from reading this book will give you
more tolerance and MORE TOOLS to do the best job you
can. This book says "dog" in the title, but Consultants for
any species will benefit from the knowledge contained in
these pages."

—Brenda Aloff, CDBC,
Author and owner of Heaven on Arf,
Positive Reinforcement: Training Dogs in the Real World;
Aggression in Dogs:
Practical Management, Prevention, and Behaviour Modification;
Canine Body Language:
Interpreting the NativeLanguage of the Domestic Dog;
Foundation Behaviours for Every Dog (DVD)

ii

"(Animal behavior consultants) are lucky to have such a resource. It is well-organized, easy to read and comprehensive without being overly wordy. It is unique. There is not anything else out there that speaks so precisely, with such intimate knowledge, about the situations animal behavior consultants deal with daily. The solid information on intervention is outstanding. This is very exciting . . ."

—Mira Jones, CDBC
Owner, *TailLights Ranch*
Flower Mound, Texas

"Lynn Hoover most certainly understands; animal behavior consultants help families. Dogs just happen to be four-legged family members. Being able to help most efficiently is all about being able to navigate family dynamics, and *The Family in Dog Behavior Consulting* explains how to do that. This topic is important and often overlooked. Lynn, a medical family therapist and dog behavior consultant, is an expert in human and canine relationships and the interplay between them. She is the perfect person to have written this excellent, groundbreaking text."

Steve Dale, CABC
Tribune Media Services syndicated
newspaper column "My Pet World," contributing editor *USA Weekend*, host Pet Central, WGN Radio (www.wgnradio.com) and
syndicated radio shows
Steve Dale's Pet World and
The Pet Minute

THE FAMILY IN DOG BEHAVIOR CONSULTING

LYNN D. HOOVER, MSW, CDBC

LEGAND PUBLISHING

iv

Grateful acknowledgement is made to the following for permission to reprint previously published material:
Monica McGoldrick, PhD and Elizabeth Carter, PhD,
The Family Lifecycle Chart

Requests for permission to reprint from book should be sent to:
Lynn Hoover
E-mail: jlrhoover@comcast.net

ISBN 0-9779949-0-2
SAN 850-8313

Editing: Beth Adelman and Rebecca Hoover
Cover design: Sheri Huffman

Legand Publishing
Production Coordinated by
Flambeau Litho Corporation

CONTENTS

Foreword by Mary Burch. Ph.D., ix

Acknowledgements, xv

I.
Introduction..1

Ten Truths, 3

The Family, 7

If I Am the Singer, You Are the Song, 8

II.
Rules, Roles and Boundaries........................11

Generational Patterns and Rules, 22

Rules for Dogs, 24

Rules that Harm Dogs, 25

Rules that Determine Role, 26

Rules about Dog Training, 27

Rules about Managing Dogs, 28

Rules and Responsibilities to Society, 30

III.

Triangles in Family Systems............................33

Typical Triangles, 40

Role of Anxiety in Triangulation, 46

Summary, 54

IV.

The Family Lifecylce......................................55

Single Young Adult, 61

The Young Couple, 63

Families with Young Children, 68

Families with Adolescents, 72

Launching Children and Moving On, 75

Families in Later Life. 80

V.

Influencing Change.......................................83

Joining, 91

Goal-Directed Interventions, 94

Focus and Separation Anxiety, 95

Reframing, 102

Enactment, 105

Interviews: Who to Include, 108

Triangulation and Cherry-Picking, 110

Intensity, 113

Boundary-Making and Unbalancing, 116

VI.
Person of the Behavior Consultant............121

The Truth about Positive Regard and Differences, 121

Personal Growth, 125

Use of Self: Empathy and Self-Awareness, 130

Values and Value Differences, 136

How We Err, 137

Social Change and Triangulation, 142

Appendix A
Study Questions, 147

Appendix B
Collaborative Healthcare Model, 153

Appendix C
Web Resources, 155

Glossary, 159

References and Suggested Reading, 163

Index, 167

FOREWORD
By
MARY BURCH, Ph.D.

Looking back on all the years I grew up with dogs, I tell people my dad was one of the original responsible pet owners. Even though we were not wealthy, our dogs were cared for extremely well. They had regular veterinary check-ups, lived in the house and were considered family members, were spayed or neutered, always had a large fenced yard, and received plenty of attention and love. When I was in college and went home to visit, I noticed that the current dog always received the same good care I remembered from years past. But, as time passed, my parents began to exhibit behavior drift with regard to the way they fed the family dog. Rather than feeding the dog once or twice a day, our waddling walrus shaped Wire Fox Terrier was getting his meals in a free feed fashion. Food, consisting of plenty of wet dog food and human food, was always present, and there were small dishes of colorful dog biscuits spread around the house "in case he got hungry."

Several years later, after I had become a professional who traveled around the country and consulted on dog-related issues, I took on the mission of improving the

nutritional plan for the dog who belonged to my
parents. By this time, I was a dog trainer, Animal
Control Officer, Certified Applied Animal Behaviorist,
and was being invited to speak on canine matters
throughout the United States and abroad. It seemed
that everyone on the planet was eager to listen to what
I had to say except my parents. Sadly, I was never able
to change their behavior with regard to the way they
fed their dogs.

When I got married, lo and behold, I discovered that
my mother-in-law had been to the same school of How
to Feed a Dog as my parents. Apparently, this generation of caring, loving people who had gone without food
during the years of The Great Depression, had developed the value system that if you really love someone,
you will see to it that he never goes hungry. My
mother-in-law also had treats, dog bowls around her
house and in addition, she woke up bright and early
every morning and cooked egg noodles to add to the
bowl for her Pekingese mix. "Snuggles likes noodles in
the morning," she would say. I shopped for high
caliber, premium dog food, brought it to her, and
talked about the right amounts of protein, fat, and
fiber for dogs. I told her about the problems that could
result when dogs were morbidly obese. I showed her
how all the soft food was causing gum disease in her
little dog. Nevertheless, as with my parents, my
credentials did not impress my in-laws and I never had
any impact. When my mother-in-law died, Snuggles
went to live with Charlie, a family friend. Due to
Snuggle's condition, I knew that it would be only a
matter of months before Charlie called to say that the
little blonde Pekingese mixed breed was gone. It
turned out, however, that Charlie was dog savvy, and
he immediately started feeding her dry kibble and a
proper diet. Within a year, Snuggles was like a new

dog who was active, happy, healthy, free of oral problems, and the proper weight.

If only I had read Lynn Hoover's book, *The Family in Dog Behavior Consulting,* I think I could have made a difference with my parents and in-laws. After reading Hoover's book, I finally understood why I was not successful in changing behavior: I was working so hard to provide information and education that I had completely overlooked the critical role that values played in these two remarkably similar situations. I did not need to buy the proper dog food or give a world-class lecture on the nutritional needs of canines; I needed to think much more about how to assess and influence change within a family.

Hoover explains family systems theory in a manner that is easy-to-understand. This highly theoretical topic could befuddle most practitioners, but Hoover uses interesting examples and cases to explain conceptual content skillfully. Early in the book, she describes rules that can harm dogs, such as the belief that if a dog bites, it should be immediately euthanized, or that larger dogs are "outside" dogs who should live their lives in the backyard. Considering that so many animal behavior consultants are working with shelter dogs, these ideas are extremely timely. With appalling numbers of animals being relinquished to shelters for health and behavior problems, we need to think less about fixing animals and more about influencing families.

The section titled "Ten Truths about Families with Problem Dogs" is honest and hard-hitting. Hoover reminds us that by the time most families contact an animal behavior consultant, they have considered letting go of their dog. Ever the optimists and not wanting to assume any guilt, families will say they will find the dog a home in the country. "The truth is," says Hoover, "there are very few homes in the country or anywhere for problem dogs."

Study objectives and a list of recommended readings are provided for this text to help readers learn the information. These helpful features make this book suitable for a course or seminar.

The Family in Dog Behavior Consulting describes a number of very practical techniques including how to use a variety of relaxers to treat dogs with separation anxiety, how to do reframing using nonjudgmental approaches, and how to enact procedures. The book also addresses the most common problems encountered by consultants who work with animals and their families. Problems with timing, behavior plans, the "My Way is Right" approach, and philosophical differences can prevent us from having positive results with animals.

A key concept for understanding family dynamics is triangulation, the tendency of two people to draw in a third person or an animal when tension develops between the two. Most animal behavior consultants deal with triangulation at one time or another, although they may not recognize it. Problems can arise between spouses when one person turns to an animal for emotional support; or when a consultant uses an approach that is too aggressive; it is not long before family members team up to undermine the consultant.

Lynn Hoover is one of the most well respected professionals in the field of animal behavior consulting. In her role as the President of the International Association of Animal Behavior Consultants (IAABC), she routinely assists individuals and small groups of consultants to determine the best course of action in consulting situations. She is a true leader who is known in professional settings for her fairness, level head, calm style, and as an exemplar for professional behavior. Throughout the book, Hoover's counseling background and leadership skills shine through with her emphasis on positive regard and respecting the opinions of others.

The numerous take-home messages in *The Family in Dog Behavior Consulting* are crucial for anyone who will be consulting with families. To help the dog, we have to help the family; so simple, yet so few consultants remember it. Ethical consultants do not try to advance their own agendas; rather, they focus on the best outcome for dogs and their owners. Moreover, we can be more effective at working with families when we understand how they function.

If we only had to work with dogs, our jobs would be easy. Many of us have said that we have a tendency to look at the wrong end of the leash when analyzing a problem. *The Family in Dog Behavior Consulting* is the first book to help us appreciate the complex dynamics at the other end of the leash. Understanding these dynamics will help us achieve the best possible outcomes for animals and their families.

—Mary R. Burch, PhD
Certified Applied Animal Behaviorist
Certified Animal Behavior Consultant
Board Certified Behavior Analyst

ACKNOWLEDGEMENTS

I set out to have someone else develop a profession for animal behavior consultants and write a book about dogs and family systems, but the responsibilities fell to me. I stayed at the plate thanks to my husband, Jim, who gives generously to the benefit of many. I thank my son, Jeff, for being his own wonderful self, steadfast, witty and kind, my brother, Allan, for his essential goodness and love, and Len Press for his extraordinary empathy and insight.

A special word of gratitude goes to my daughter, Rebecca, deeply compassionate and aware, and always ready for another adventure. She did a great deal to make this text ready for publication, including editing.

Thanks also to friends Veronica Sanchez and Niki Lamproplos for the laughter and steady support, editor extraordinaire Beth Adelman, and acclaimed scholar Mary Burch for believing in my book and sharing my vision for the profession. Carrots for retired police horse, Donald Duck, powerful in heart and mind. Kudos to Carole Duffy who believed in him and many times saved him.

Many thanks to the Board of Directors of the International Association of Animal Behavior Consultants (IAABC) for their integrity, solid strength, and fidelity to mission: Pam Johnson-Bennett, Chris Hamer, Debbie Winkler, Beth Adelman, Chris Bach, Ilene Nathan, Mira Jones, Liz Wilson, and Debbie Strother. Finally, I deeply appreciate the Founding Members of the IAABC:

The characteristic of heroism

Is indeed persistency, and tolerance is a virtue[1]

---

[1] Adapted from a Ralph Waldo Emerson quote

The Family
in Dog Behavior
Consulting

"There is a tendency for living things to join up, establish linkages, live inside each other, return to earlier arrangements, get along whenever possible. This is the way of the world."

~ *Lewis Thomas,*
Lives of a Cell

Chapter 1:
INTRODUCTION

Ten Truths
About Families
with "Problem" Dogs

1. Dogs with resolvable behavior problems are being inappropriately punished, discarded and euthanized—in droves! It is consistent with social norms for families not to expend much energy on their dogs and to give up easily.

2. It is difficult for most owners to figure out where they will find competent help for animals with issues, and there is a need for thousands more qualified behavior consultants, trainers, behaviorists, and veterinary behaviorists than are currently available.

3. By the time most families who have dogs with issues find their way to a qualified behavior professional, they have considered getting rid of their dog.

4. A message behavior professionals often hear is, "If you cannot help us we will try to find her a home in the country." The truth is, of course, there are very few homes in the country, or anywhere, for problem dogs.

5. When it concerns dog behavior, everyone is an expert—grandparents, the neighbors, veterinarians, groomers, and salespeople in pet stores. By the time a real expert shows up, for many families they are just another person with a point of view.

6. Most families start out planning not to invest much time or money in behavior consulting or training.

7. Dog behavior consultants work with families more successfully when they know something about how families function and dysfunction, how they solve problems, and how their attempted solutions sometimes make things worse. Families who are not effective problem-solvers do not suddenly become good problem-solvers just because we are there to help them.

8. We are committed to helping families enjoy their dogs and have mutually satisfying relationships with them. This is a great "selling point" and avenue for entry with families.

9. Many dog's behavior problems can be successfully resolved, and more can be adequately managed so dogs can have reasonable lives with their families.

10. Families contract with us to bring about change in their dogs. We are not family counselors, but, the truth is, to help their dogs, families have to change too.

The Family

The family provides the principal relational and social context in which many aspects of a dog's behavior are formed. Families can become either assets or liabilities in this process. A basic understanding of family systems theory will assist dog behavior consultants in their work. We can learn to evaluate how the functioning of client families affects dogs, and to select interventions that provide a better outcome for dogs. Completely new interventions come to mind when we look at families as systems and dogs as symptom-bearers for families and active participants in family dramas.

We typically use the term "family" to refer to traditional social groups with one or two parents and their children. However, a family system, the unit that we are tending to here, can be an individual, an owner living alone with dogs, a couple, or an extended family going back several generations with members both living and deceased. Even the man living isolated on an island has images and memories of family. He went to the island to escape, but discovers that they continue to inhabit his lonely mind. Perhaps they are still telling him what to do.

This book gives more than an overview but less than a full exploration of each construct. The systems concepts that are described in the following pages are complex. They cannot be understood with one reading. I suggest that you re-read the text a minimum of three times or listen to the audio CDs. Read the two books by Dr. Salvador Minuchin and H. Charles Fishman listed in "Recommended Reading," and respond to study questions in the appendix at the end of the book to enhance your learning.

If I Am the Singer, You Are the Song . . .

As self-contained individuals, you and I have unique characteristics that remain stable over time. Perhaps you are artistic and I have a flare for creative writing. I do not multi-task well and you cannot spell. We both have intelligence quotients that endure over time. We love animals, especially dogs.

However, other portions of our "selves" are fluid, moving back and forth, in and out of tune with our environments with each person or situation we encounter eliciting different aspects of ourselves. I might be gentle and a peacemaker with my colleagues but become a lioness in defense of my family. You might become rejecting when you do not get your way, or only when you feel threatened by someone who holds values different from your own. I might become testy if you block my ability to get things done.

Similarly, a portion of each dog's behavior is stable. For example, some dogs are more easily aroused and do not react well to novel stimuli. Others are easily aroused but can adjust to the new and unexpected. Some dogs guard precious possessions and others are naturals at offering them up freely, regardless of training. Nevertheless, dogs also evidence behaviors that are rooted in context, with the dog acting and reacting to environmental stimuli.

Dogs are especially influenced by humans in the families with which they live, and similarly influence their humans' responses to them. For example, a dog with a fearful human handler may develop fears and phobias to rival those of her owner (through *owner reinforcement*). A hyperactive dog who is punished for misbehavior may become more anxious and destructive as a result. It is clear that dogs cannot be fully understood without also considering them within the context of their families. "If I am the singer, you are the song" says the dog with behavior problems.

For a complete picture, we must consider systemic and environmental influences. A dog's behavior is affected by her relationships with owners, groomers, veterinarians, neighbors, delivery persons, trainers and consultants, other animals, and objects in the environment (placement of the crate in relation to humans and placement of the food bowl in relation to other animals' food, etc.) . . . and our behavior is affected by the dog. Thus, the question for us as behavior consultants becomes, "What do we need to know about the relationships between dog, family, and environment, to help us formulate accurate and usable assumptions about dogs?" Our next question must be, "What should we then do about it?"

In the first sections, we look at key concepts that help us conceptually: rules, roles, and boundaries, and triangles and triangulation. Then we go on to the stages in the family lifecycle, interventions that dog behavior consultants can use to improve lives, and finally, the person of the consultant. ■

Chapter 2

RULES, ROLES AND BOUNDARIES

Fans of J.R.R. Tolkien will appreciate the analogies that follow. Most Americans embrace the value of self-determination and hold in high regard rugged individualists such as Aragorn in Tolkien's *Lord of the Rings*. But did Aragorn, as a descendent of kings, come out of his mother's womb with the powerful personal qualities he evidenced in his brave defense of Middle Earth? Or did his childhood with elf king Elrond and the elves of Rivendell shape his character and values? Surely, Aragorn's formation resulted from a mixture of nature and nurture. So it is with humans and their dogs.

According to Dr. Nathan Ackerman, grandfather of the family therapy movement, families have the capacity to both stifle and enhance the full range of human experience. Tolkien's Aragorn loved deeply and had friends he could trust. He came and went as duty called and worked his way into a full expression of self as leader of Men. He did so with impetus from Elrond. Arwen, daughter of Elrond, further sustained Aragorn with her love and Elvish power. The systems in which

Aragorn immersed himself—family, Arwen, the Fellowship—collectively brought out the best in him; he was also good for them. Aragorn reached his fullest potential as the rightful ruler of Middle Earth after successfully defeating the enemy. All of the Fellowship matured along with him during their long journey.

Actor Viggo Mortensen had this to say about his character Aragorn's relationship with Arwen: "The thing that stands out for me is they both feel their union is more profound and long-lasting than their individual existences could ever be. They have each other in mind. They've known for a long time that they're much better together than they are apart."[1]

Aragorn benefited from his relationship with other powerful figures, such as Elrond and the wizard Gandalf. Thus, Aragorn's presentation of self was shaped through exchanges with associates, friends, and family who were also open to the fullness of life. Aragorn received much support from his respective social systems and therefore was able to actualize himself to the fullest. Aragorn even brought out the best in his horse.

On the flip side, some social systems are stifling. We have all been in environments where we feel that we cannot present ourselves as we really are. Maybe no one asks about the real us and it seems as if they do not care. This is a regular occurrence in some families. Similarly, in one family it might be all right to mention that we are having a problem, but only after we have found a solution. In other families, members can

---

[1] From the *Lord of the Rings Interviews*: *How do you see the relationship between Aragorn and Arwen? (Arwen helps Aragorn to embrace his destiny)*. Web: www.lordoftherings.net

chatter endlessly about problems and are never expected to solve them. In these families, problem solving is not a goal.

The stifling of the range of human expression can actually be functional in some settings, even as it leaves us feeling as if we are gasping for breath. In a work setting, for example, it might reasonably be expected that employees leave personal problems at the door. Similarly, during a crisis, family members will often submerge feelings for the good of the system.

Families similarly limit their dog's presentation of self, and we all know that what is best for families is not always best for dogs. How many dogs have you worked with whom you suspect would flourish in another environment but do not adapt well to the environment they are in? Perhaps the developmental stage of the family is what is making the match incompatible, but just as often it is the rules or boundaries set by the system that prevent dogs from being their own best selves and stop family members from responding to legitimate needs.

To illustrate, I worked with a Toy Poodle who had been turned in to a rescue group for snarling, snapping, and finally biting her owners. Our challenge was to decide if she could be successfully rehomed. We noted that her whole demeanor changed when we had her in a *right relationship* with her humans. With some investigation, we discovered that the husband in the dog's former family had issues with anger and disliked the dog, while the wife was stressed and not emotionally available. Does it surprise you that the dog did not appear to feel safe? We managed to rehome her successfully, with a confident and nurturing woman. The Toy Poodle with a "bite history" quickly became a companion of the finest kind, with the owner serving faithfully as loving caretaker and guide. We changed the environment, relationship, and rules, and the dog responded beautifully, presumably, because her needs were being met.

Rules are more than a set of expectations that families use to govern members' actions. Rules define who may participate and how. For example, in some families children should be seen but not heard. The child who advances original ideas at the dinner table might be considered rude. Rules, or boundaries, also dictate what the consequences will be for certain actions. Also, the child who "thinks too much of herself" might be "put in her place" by parents and siblings. Indeed, humility stems from recognizing one's limitations, and some families are more proficient (and zealous) than others at pointing out limitations. Similarly, a dog who clamors to have his needs met might go without because he has been dismissed by his family as "spoiled" or "dominant".

Rules serve as norms that regulate members' behavior and keep systems stable. Families tend to interact in repetitious sequences. They are governed by a small set of patterned and predictable rules. Indeed, the system that changes its rules around too often creates anxiety in members, who furtively cast about trying to figure out what is expected of them. We all know of children in more contentious families who complain, "No matter what I do, I can never please mother," meaning, in this example, that mother is shifty about her wants so family members are left in a perpetual state of not knowing how to please her. These types of ever-changing patterns are energy-sappers; the functional mother who is dedicated to preserving family resources will make her wants known in a more straightforward manner.

Family members do not have as much invested emotionally in their dogs as they do in each other. They are generally clear with us about what they want. However, what if they are unclear with each other about who should be doing what to help the dog? What if relationship issues among extended family is effecting how members process information about their dogs?

I have colleagues who are knowledgeable, reliable, and proficient trainers. They complain because their siblings or parents routinely toss aside their advice and do the exact wrong thing. For example, one trainer I know warned her sister and her husband against buying from a pet store or adopting from a rescue group that does not screen for behavioral issues. The couple was ready for a dog and set out armed with this knowledge. In the end, they brought home two dogs. One was a busier than usual older puppy from a pet store who promised to grow very big (though their yard was small and their possibilities for meeting the pup's exercise needs were limited). The other was a dog who picked the sister and her husband out at a shelter. (He wagged his tail, obviously happy to see them.) The couple did not ask if the dog had behavioral issues and did not discover "problem areas" (resource guarding, leash aggression) until he had been in their home for a few weeks. Did compassion blind the couple to reality? Are they just contrary people by nature? Perhaps. We know that emotional forces in families also drive decision-making. In other words, if a neighbor had given the couple an article to read on responsible adoption, would the sister and her spouse have paid attention and avoided the grief that comes from adopting two dogs that they could not live with comfortably, long-term? Would the dogs have been spared a lengthy experience with owners who did not have the resources to move them in healthy directions?

A few years ago, I attended a summer celebration for a friend's extended family, with all the generations represented. The families were known to be competitive and I will posit that competitive people (as a generational pattern) do not make good relatives because they are not concerned with deepening emotional ties. Relationships do not go far with people locked in competitive patterns because their goal is to establish themselves as better. They might even compete with their dogs, or perchance choose the company of dogs over humans because they do not feel they have to compete with them! Thus, on a warm summer's day I paid special attention to the family's interplay over dogs and took note when one couple tied their dog to a tree in a shady spot where she would get a lot of attention. I observed that the dog had been resting there for just five minutes when an older generation couple brought her a bowl filled with water. If I had not known that this family was invested in maintaining a certain hierarchy in a pattern that extended through the generations, I would have thought the relatives wanted to make sure the dog was not thirsty. However, I knew that this family's benevolence usually had a kick to it. So, was the giving of water yet another, comparatively innocent example of one-upsmanship, a subtle suggestion that the water-bearers were better caretakers of dogs than the dog's owners were? The water was carried in full view of the extended family, who presumably had not been counting the minutes and might possibly have concluded that the dog's owners were negligent—which they were not.

In the example above, the dog was at least getting her needs met. In some families who are concerned with hierarchy, or rank, dogs might be relegated to the bottom of the totem pole, the last to eat and drink. A family could withhold water at night even if their dog appears thirsty because they fear the dog will ask to be let out while they are sleeping. Claiming to have a unique understanding of dogs, they might say, "She's not thirsty!" with authority when the dog appears to even a non-expert to be searching for water.

Explicit and implicit rules

Are rules obvious to family members and observers, such as dog behavior consultants? Yes and no. Sometimes the family will tell you, "Oh, we would never do that" when your suggestion violates their rules for personal or familial behavior. Other times a family will say "yes" because your ideas ring true and what you propose will obviously solve their problem . . . but their "no" actions speak to an implicit—or hidden—rule against the activity you have outlined for them. For example, suppose your client is a couple who relies on an electronic system to contain their dog, and their dog recently bit a delivery person from behind. You are certain that there is a link between the dog's apparent anxiety over the electronic collar and the bite. You present this "truth" in a straightforward manner and the family seems to go along with your plan to stop using the collar. However, minus a containment system, they will have to walk the dog or install a fence. You do not know this yet, but they also have medical issues that preclude walks. In addition, the family has already spent more than expected on the dog for veterinary care and they do not intend to spend for any more than routine costs and a few hours for your services. The implicit rule is that they have just about reached their limit on costs for the dog and they will extend themselves no further.

What could you do to improve the outcome for the dog in a situation such as the one just described? First, do not move in too quickly with what seems to you to be an obvious solution. You should ask questions; get to know the family and their real-life possibilities and limitations. As you introduce ideas, solicit feedback so you know if the family is truly with you.

I worked with a couple in a situation similar to the one described above. They would not and could not put in a physical fence. If the electronic apparatus was gone, the dog would have to go too. However, I was able to introduce interventions that so improved the relationship between the owners and the dog, and between the dog and the fence, that the dog no longer aggressed when strangers came on his property. (Central to the plan, we reinforced the dog for running to his owner whenever he felt afraid. Interestingly, the owner had thought the dog was being "dominant" so had rebuffed the dog's previous attempts to go to him for protection.) If I had imposed a rigid rule that said, "I am not working with you unless you scrap the electronic containment system" what would my being "right" or "holding the higher moral ground" have accomplished for this dog? Should we have tried for rehoming? He had a bite history so groups and shelters would not have taken him. My job is not to advance my own agenda but to bring about the best among *possible* outcomes for dogs and owners.

Tolerance for differences

Another area of interest is the level of agreement and tolerance for differences among family members. Are diversity and different viewpoints acceptable, or is only "our way" tolerated? Some families impose a rule on members that says, "We must agree on every value." Other families say it is acceptable to agree only on key values.

As an example, in my family it is acceptable for members of all generations to disagree on almost any issue, and it is expected that we will not personalize disputes. Therefore, a family member or visitor might say, "I don't agree and here is why," or, "I agree with point A but am not with you on point B." A family member would not say (implicitly or explicitly), "What is wrong with you? How could you think that?" or, "I don't want anything more to do with you if that is the opinion you hold!" There are caveats to our free-speech rule, however: "Don't upset Grandma by telling her what you think [about controversial issues]." Also, "If you have anything nice to say about George W. Bush, don't discuss politics with Uncle Allan!" All members are expected to adhere to the value that accords respect for differences. Conversely, some family members want a committed life—that is, with commitments to causes larger than themselves—and others want a comfortable life. Members are free to choose along the continuum between the two values, though there is some friction between those farthest apart on the poles that separate altruism from misanthrope.

Good-enough families

Good-enough families are problem-solvers. They are open to differences and able to process new information. They meet members' essential needs and support each individual's growth along the developmental continuum.

Now, do we prefer working with more open families, with whom it is evident that different points of view can be expressed, or with closed families who block our expression of self? Of course, we prefer the former because they are willing to think about their dog in new ways. In addition, they will try interventions that take them in directions not previously considered. If they are essentially closed to new information, we have to work that much harder to get information through.

Adaptive patterns facilitate novel and creative forms of problem solving. Another way of saying this is that some families are more effective problem solvers because their members are free to find their way to workable solutions. Less functional families are apt to stay faithful to old ways that do not work. The world is changing around them but they cannot change with the change. We have an ethical obligation to try to facilitate movement so we can fulfill our mission to help dogs and dog-family relationships.

Open vs. closed systems

My own family is a reasonably open system, although we do have areas of closure. Overall, we value a broad spectrum of human beings and they do not have to be just like us to earn our respect. In addition, we teach members to look for the good in people and recognize that we all contribute to the pot. We value our way and it works for us, but ours is not the only way. Family members are expected to look for new information to inform their choices.

In some families, new information is not as welcome and family members are expected to appear to be knowledgeable, even if they are not. Members of families who prefer closure might be insulted or repelled by the introduction of new information. That is, if we try to tell them "the truth" and the truth is different from their preferred explanations, they will likely reject it and us. Perhaps they believe, for example, that dogs who assert themselves with humans are trying to dominate and we tell them the dog just wants something; instead of savoring the insights, they may decide that we do not know as much as they do about dogs.

Most of us have worked with families with resource-guarding dogs who tell us that their dogs are trying to dominate them. We can challenge the notion of dominance and talk about the problem from the dog's "it's mine!" point of view. Some families yield right away to our assessment and we are confident that we will be able to help them. Other families do not surrender as easily to more complex explanations of dog behavior. If they appear to be unwilling to give up the idea that their dogs want to "dominate," it will be because their ideas about dominance serve a function in the family system. They might not wish to think of themselves as unnecessarily harsh, so they cling to the idea that they owe it to the dog to show him who is boss. Alternatively, perhaps a family member has a need to control and expresses it through his "dominant" dog who he orders around and then, for emphasis, alpha rolls.

When I could see no way around dominance constructs, I have actually agreed with owners. "Maybe
you are right and dogs do need to be dominated."
Nevertheless, why be so dramatic about it? We ask our
dogs to sit and they submit when they sit. If dogs do
not sit as instructed, we simply withhold rewards until
they defer. If the owners are using aversives or otherwise "getting tough", they are not dominating correctly. I ask if they want me to show them modern
techniques. The strategy I just described is called
"reframing," and I will explain it in detail in chapter
five on influencing change

If a family does not accept our reality, we must first
consider that their hesitation might be justified.
Perhaps our assessment is off-target or our explanations are fuzzy. However, if we have confidence in our
ideas and members continue to resist, we can suspect
families have issues with information processing and
their preferred explanations meet some needs, not
necessarily for the dog but for them.

Generational Patterns and Rules

The consultant who figures out what the generational
patterns and rules are in a family is in a strong position to target interventions and achieve change.

We need look no further than our own families to see
behavioral sequences that define character and func-
tionality. These patterns are passed along from one
generation to the next. Do you recognize yourself in
any of the following?

➤ A child-centered family, where the parents tend better to their children than to their own relationship until the children are launched.

➤ A child-centered family that holds on to their grown children when they should be letting go.

➤ A family of divorce. Subsequent generations are more likely to divorce because they have not inherited a pattern for working through problems.

➤ Parents who are particularly good at teaching personal responsibility and the work ethic but avoid discussing relationship issues.

➤ Parents who offer a legacy of giving to the less fortunate.

➤ Families who value communicative intimacy; that is, they talk openly about their feelings and concerns.

➤ Parents in blue-collar jobs who prepare their children for blue-collar jobs. The message is, "Imitate us."

➤ Parents with low income and education levels who push their children to do better than them by going to college. The message is, "Always do the best you can with what you have."

Rules about outsiders

Some families are more welcoming and inclusive than others. An open family might agree to compassionate rules such as, "If you don't have anything nice to say about someone, look harder until you find something worth commending." Other families are harsh. They will join to condemn outsiders who get into conflicts with individual members.

In less open families, members are expected to draw from the system for support. If a member looks for too many solutions outside the family, he will be considered disloyal.

I imagine that we have all worked with families who listen to what we say as if they have heard it all before. Alternatively, the parental subsystem has to be always "in the know." Either way, they will tend to hear what we say as identical or similar to something they heard before, especially if they believe they are experts on dogs. Knowledge is power. We can sometimes squeak just enough information through to dislodge families from rigid patterns so dogs can make more satisfactory adjustments.

Rules for Dogs

We have established that families are governed by rules and that some of the rules they set for themselves apply to dogs. Rules are usually passed down through the generations, with some modification when new information about dogs becomes known. Dog behavior consultants are the purveyors of new information, and as such, we have a unique opportunity to improve upon generational patterns that affect the welfare of dogs.

Examples of rules that harm dogs

> ➤ Dogs must not react unfavorably to anything humans do to them.

> ➤ Dogs must not growl at humans, ever.

> ➤ Dogs must not bite anyone except robbers . . . and possibly Uncle Harry!

> ➤ Dogs who disobey are trying to dominate and must be put in their place.

> ➤ Dogs who bite should not be allowed to live.

> ➤ The least expensive grocery store kibble is good enough for dogs.

> ➤ Dogs should be made to do things that other dogs do, even if they are scared.

Rules about roles

Dog owners exercise some choice over the roles dogs play in families. Dogs may be there for utilitarian purposes only. They hunt, herd, guard, or protect. If dogs do not satisfy their intended purposes, they can be discarded. Other dogs are more fortunate. They have families who allow them to flourish at their "personal best." For example, the one-person dog might be given a special someone to devote her whole self to, while the social dog is welcome to join in family activities and make friends wherever he goes.

Social norms help to define roles. The dog who herds cattle might be valued by the farmer for his skill, but the farmer does not enter into a personal relationship with the dog. However, these days, most American families appreciate the immediate and long-term value of companion animals and there is a well-developed body of research that is demonstrating that companion animals are good for our health.

> *Dogs are perfect at being dogs—*
> *Dogs are perfect at being themselves.*
> *~ Chris Bach*

Rules that determine the role dogs can assume in families

➢ Our dog is a member of our family and we will do everything we can to see that she remains with us.

➢ Dogs are dirty and belong outside.

➢ The dog's needs will be met last.

➢ Mom's dog comes first.

➢ It is okay for the women in the family to dote on dogs, but not the men.

➢ A family owes dogs affection and attention.

➢ Dogs are living creatures and must be protected.

➤ All we owe a dog is food, water, and a soft bed.

➤ Big dogs are dirty, little dogs belong with us.

➤ We believe in the healing power of pets.

➤ A dog must not reflect badly on us.

Rules about dog training

➤ A dog should want to please us.

➤ Any dog with a good character will do what we want because he loves us. We are not giving our dogs cookies for good behavior! You say punishment is the only alternative? We are still not using treats.

➤ Our feeling is that dogs should do what we want because we say so.

➤ Positive reinforcement trainers use head halters, so head halters are good. My dog hates his head halter, but he will get used to it. Head halters are good.

➤ If my dog dislikes a training tool, it is not the right training tool for my dog. Out goes the tool!

➤ Electronic collars, choke, and prong collars are evil and must never be used on dogs, by anyone.

➤ If the dog gets loose, run after him!

> ➢ Men are the problem solvers for dogs. (What if the consultant is a woman?)

Family and societal rules further determine what tasks the owners will take care of themselves for the dog and what tasks they will share with others, such as a trainer or a behavior consultant. Some tasks will be handed over to others completely, such as veterinary care, grooming, or boarding.

We have all worked with families who take their reactive dogs to groomers and the dogs are stressed. Nevertheless, the grooming goes on and on . . . until the dog finally aggresses. The owners and groomers expect that dogs should be able to hold up for grooming, no matter what their genetic predisposition or life experience. They do not make allowances for breed differences because they believe that one breed should be able to hold up as well as another, and if not, the deficiency is in the dog, not in their approach. What does it say about dogs that they can be put in highly stressful situations from which there is no escape, repeatedly, and yet many do not aggress?

Rules about managing dogs

> ➢ Whoever wakes first should let the puppy out or be prepared to clean up!

> ➢ Nobody should upset the dog!

> ➢ Keep the gate latched so the dog does not escape.

> ➢ Children learn responsibility by caring for the family dog. Therefore, parents will not share in the dog's care. If the children fail, the dog goes.

> Children learn responsibility by caring for dogs. Therefore, parents will not assist in caring for them. When the children fail, though, mom fills in. But, don't tell dad!

> We do not want our dogs on medication.

> Dogs should know better than to leave the yard.

> Grandma's dog tried to bite me! If she keeps that dog, I'm not going to visit her ever again!

> It is a very serious problem if the dog eliminates in the house!

> Our dog knows he was not supposed to run off. He is in big trouble when he gets home!

> Crates are good, positive reinforcement trainers use them. Therefore, leaving our dog in a crate all day is okay. He is safe there.

> We do not believe in crates, even for house-training. However, if our dog keeps peeing in the house he is going to have to leave.

> Dogs are never allowed on the furniture— except when the parents are not at home!

Rules that relate to the owner's sense of responsibility to society

> Dogs who bark are public nuisances. We want to be good neighbors so we will not leave our dog out when he is barking.

> If our dog barks, the neighbors will just have to put up with it.

> Dogs who growl and show aggression are not bad, but it is our responsibility to protect others from bites.

> If our dog bites them, it is their own fault. Especially if we have warned them to leave him alone!

> Dogs need opportunities to run free. If this upsets people, they will have to get over it!

When we are working with potentially dangerous dogs, we unquestionably must assess their families too. Are they families we can trust to keep their dogs out of trouble? Can we count on them to protect the public? The prognosis for an aggressive dog living with an unreliable family is not nearly as good as the prognosis for a dog living with a responsible family whose judgment is sound. We admit to needing motivated families. However, what we really need is *protective* families who will work hard.

When dogs are stressed

The much larger problem for dogs, of course, is that dogs who have been mismanaged and otherwise provoked by their humans to bite wind up with bite histories, and are not wanted anywhere, even in shelters. We have to get to families *before* their dogs are so stressed that they resort to biting.

When dogs are stuck

Most dogs get to live indoors with their families, to their obvious benefit. However, there can be downsides: In modern America, dogs are more tightly controlled than ever and are less able to escape dysfunctional family patterns and ill-suited rules. ■

Chapter 3:

TRIANGLES IN FAMILY SYSTEMS

"The self of the blind man includes the

ground he is walking on."

~ Salvador Minuchin, M.D.

Do you ever notice what happens when tensions begin to rise between you and another person? Perhaps you launch into a discussion with a friend, expecting that you and she will have the same perspective, but discover that you have less in common than you realized. Your friend looks uncomfortable, and you sense that she is not responding favorably to your ideas. Casting about, you hit upon a way to salvage the situation. *Triangulation!* That is, you are able to restore equilibrium, to calm things down, by referring to a third person whose ideas are even less appealing. The two of you may reunite against that third person, who has the misfortune of not being present to create his own exculpatory triangle.

For example, say you are meeting for the first time with a dog groomer who regularly refers clients to you but does not know your training philosophy. You start talking about your favorite training treats and she launches into a diatribe against "cookie pushing." She believes dogs should do what we want because we ask them to. Not wishing to lose a referral source, you join with her by complaining about trainers who push treats at dogs but do not actually get them trained. As a result, the groomer is looking down on the "real cookie pushers" and has forgotten her initial perception that you were one of them. Now, if this is how you handle your differences, chances are you will go home feeling not so good about yourself. The higher integrity response would be to discuss the use of treats with the groomer, objectively and without apology—without resorting to triangulation.

Triangulation can serve more constructive purposes than satisfying the togetherness needs of a duo at the expense of a third party or distant ideology. In better-functioning families, members negotiate issues through triangulation but succeed in shifting alignments flexibly, depending on the issue. For example, a wife may feel that a dog's place is indoors, as a loved member of the family, while the husband was raised to believe that dogs should be relegated to the yard. The wife wins support from a child, and together they assert that it is "cruel" to leave a dog outdoors. The problem is resolved when the husband relents. He may even grow to enjoy having the dog in the house.

The child hopes to press "togetherness" and "compassionate care of animals" a step further by sharing his bedroom with the dog. The mother, who is the primary housekeeper, worries about dirt. However, the father has grown fond of the dog and now remembers how, as a child, he used to sneak his outdoor dog inside and under the covers of his bed on cold nights. The child knows this, and so armed, turns to the father for support. He wins his father over, and the mother relents.

In this family, the triangles are flexible. The husband and wife are, we will posit, more often the team with the stronger voice, but the son is able to join with his father or mother at opportune times to further a "good cause."

A dysfunctional pattern is at work when an alliance becomes fixed, dominant, and inflexible. In stable coalitions, one member is consistently in alliance with another member of the household, and a third member is emotionally entrenched too, but typically on the outside. Another form of stable coalition is the *detouring coalition,* characterized by its intent to defuse stress between members by designating another party as the source of their problem and assuming an attacking or solicitous attitude toward that person. It may work, and reinforcement is all the coalition (often a couple) needs to continue using that person—or dog!—as a scapegoat. As an example, you have probably heard the old maxim, "The only thing two dog trainers can agree on is how awful a third dog trainer is." Being against a third person does not facilitate problem solving or anything productive. The third trainer, on the outside, is most often a "player" too; he might feed information to the twosome that ensures that he will be central to their discussions. Negative attention can be better than no attention at all. Family relationships are more intense, and when two consistently join against a third, they can bring to a halt the third's emergence and growth in the system and perhaps impede their own forward movement as well.

The concept of the triangle and the process of triangulation are central to the application of family systems theory to animal behavior consulting. As described in the above examples, triangulation refers to the tendency of two-person systems to draw in a third person—or an animal—when tension develops between the two. Sometimes, one of the original pair will seek to turn that third party against the other; the third party may find it necessary, for whatever reason, to cooperate first with one and then the other of the opposing parties.

The "third" might be an animal, who will be stressed by the competing expectations of the relationship system. To illustrate, a single parent mother called me in to help with a rambunctious one-year-old Labrador Retriever who was pulling on leash and jumping on people. The mother had adopted the dog to provide companionship for her early adolescent son. We sought to teach the dog self-control, but our progress was undermined because the son loved coming home from school and having the dog jump up and give him an "I'm ecstatic that I get to see you again!" greeting. In addition, the teen was in conflict with his mother, whom he thought was "a control freak." He transferred his resentment and sympathies to the dog who, as he saw it, was being over-controlled by the mother. Accordingly, he encouraged the dog to "express himself freely."

Another dynamic with the Labrador is that the son's father had died. It takes many years for children to work through the loss of a parent, and some never do. The son did not want his mother in the lead; he wanted his father as leader and role model. With these emotional forces raging, he resisted his mother's leadership even more. This was a triangle between the son, mother, and absent father. The father in this example is the "ghost," not able to be there but none-theless present in the minds of family members. Another way of saying this is that the son resisted the mother so he could keep the spot open for his father, even though he understood intellectually that his father was never coming back.

How do these complexities relate to our work as dog behavior consultants? I understood what was going on and structured my interventions to interrupt the cycle between mother, son, and dog. It was simple. I sug-gested that the mother back off and let the son do the problem solving. I met with the son without the mother present and he quickly agreed that the jump-ing up was a problem for visitors. I asked him what he thought we could do to elicit more civilized behavior from his Labrador. In this way, I extended an invita-tion to the son to step into his father's shoes and take the lead with the dog. The son asked for input from me, as a leader would, and settled on a plan. He asked his mother to support the plan: He would teach the dog to sit for greetings, and when sitting was solid, he would then teach the dog to jump up in response to the command "UP, UP, UP." He would use the "UP, UP, UP" command to elicit the familiar greeting from the dog after school. The enthusiastic greeting was only for the enjoyment of son and dog. No one but the son was to use the command. Our strategy worked, the bouncy Labrador toned down sufficiently, and both mother and son were proud of their accomplishments.

At various points, we, as consultants, become the "third" leg in triangles. The conflict or potential for conflict exists between dog owners and behavior consultants, veterinarians, groomers, rescue workers, relatives, or neighbors. Likewise, we do get asked to work with families who have an agenda other than simply helping their dog.

I had an unusual case with a happy outcome for the dog and its owners; a couple whose children were grown and out of the home. The husband called me to say that his beloved dog had bitten him. The dog already had a bad reputation at the veterinarian's, where he had "danger, aggressive, will bite" written on many pages of his chart. He was being treated for a seizure disorder, but the diagnosis, from what I could see, was not firmly established. Thyroid testing yielded marginal results.

When I arrived at the home, the dog tried to interact with me but the wife kept telling him to go lie down and leave me alone. I was grateful that she showed me how she intrudes on the dog's relationships with outsiders, but I regretted that I could not see how the dog moves on his own. The husband would say to his wife, "She [the consultant] wants to see what he does, stop intruding" and I would agree politely. The wife would stop for about a minute and then mindlessly interfere with the dog's natural movement again. So we had our triangles: wife, dog, and me . . . wife, husband, and dog . . . wife, dog, and veterinarian—for it was the wife who took the dog to the veterinarian and suffered the embarrassment of having the office staff afraid of him because he growled and snapped at them.

The dog was pleasant enough with me, even welcoming, until I brought my hand to his side. I suspected that the dog might have an undiagnosed medical condition. When I inquired, I learned that the family had been treating the dog for several months for an ear infection. The wife held up the ear medication for me to see. She said that when she tried to apply it, the dog growled and moved away from her. The job was so unpleasant that the husband never did it. I was struck by how much medicine remained in the container. I did not say the obvious: maybe he still has an ear infection. If they were thinking about euthanasia, I worried about what would happen to him if we went back to the veterinary practice where he had a "bad reputation" and was expected to arrive in a muzzle, which the couple never managed to get on him. Instead, I facilitated a referral to a different veterinarian who was known for his love of dogs and the ability to get along with most of them. The new veterinarian ran tests, took the dog off the seizure medication, and diagnosed an ear infection in the same ear that had been treated with too little medication. He gave the owners ear medicine that was easier to administer, to ensure compliance. When the dog recovered from his ear infection, he stopped growling and did not bite again.

You might rightly ask, what is so unusual about this scenario? Many dogs have undiagnosed medical conditions that affect behavior. What is different here is that I was aware of the propensity of the couple to triangulate, albeit gently. I sensed that there was tension between the couple over the husband's dog, for whom the wife did the "drudge" work. The dog had a reputation with the veterinarian's office that could have doomed him. Therefore, I decided not to point to the most obvious evidence in the room: The medication for the ears was four months old and there was a lot left, so the owners must not have been doing their job. Remember, I could not be sure the dog still had the ear infection and I knew that the couple had reservations about their usual veterinarian. For that reason, I opted to push for a new alliance with a reliable veterinarian who might help them view their dog more favorably and figure out what was ailing him. Relationships can be complicated. I run into the husband and dog at the park from time to time. It has been a year since the dog was aggressive. The dog goes willingly to the new veterinarian with no need for a muzzle.

Typical Triangles

Do you ever wonder why some families do not follow through with your carefully constructed training plans? Perhaps the family does not have the time, the energy, or is confused. Your plan could be off-target. In your search for explanations, however, do not overlook the possibility that a family's failure to comply may be motivated by relationship needs.

Perhaps the most familiar triangles are those that fit cultural norms. For example, the wife may be appropriately concerned for the dog, while the husband is more distant and harder to engage. The behavior consultant might conclude that the wife cares for the dog and the husband does not. On the contrary, it may be that the wife is the "carrier" of the couple's concern for their dog. That is, perhaps the husband would like to dote on the dog but was raised to believe that "real men" do not fuss over dogs, so the wife expresses caring on his behalf. Dogs can fare well in families with this pattern; hence, it is not something that generally has to be fixed.

In another arrangement, a couple may discover that they can avoid their own conflict over issues that have nothing to do with a dog by rallying in a united front of mutual concern for their dog. As long as they are focused on the animal's "issues," there is peace between them. If the animal's problems are settled, what is the couple left with but unresolved interpersonal issues? If they lack coping skills, they may be motivated to undermine the animal's progress rather than work through marital issues.

Of course, triangulation can be benign. Couples who frequently squabble over a pet or a child's behavior problems, may respond productively as allies when a real problem arises.

Another scenario involves couples at war. They are able to let go of their conflict when they unite to blame, or scapegoat, the family pet. This is a common occurrence, with the spouses swapping stories about the misbehaviors of the "bad" pet and their unsuccessful efforts to rehabilitate her.

Animals suffer other woes with families. As a child, I encountered a family with a Houdini cat who ran off whenever he got the chance. The family joined routinely to chase after him and when he finally allowed himself to be caught, they punished him. In this way, the family, perhaps inadvertently, guaranteed that the problem would continue and that the searches would be long and challenging. You may find yourself wondering why families still use punishment when it clearly is not helping. Even as a child, I understood that sometimes the family needs the problem more than the solution.

Similarly, we encounter owners who are kind but inept at fixing problems with their animal. If they remain incompetent in spite of our best efforts, we might suspect triangulation. Again, the need for an animal with problems can outweigh the need for problem resolution.

Suppose a child brings home a bad report card. The family has a rule that the dog is not allowed on the furniture. The child knows that his father is due home.

Accordingly, he invites the dog to find a comfortable spot for himself on the couch. When the father arrives home, the dog is "caught" and the father focuses on the dog's misbehavior. While mildly scolding the dog, he "forgets" to discuss with his son the drop in grades. The father does not enjoy confrontations. In this scenario, both parties collude, possibly unaware, to divert attention from the  real issue of the child's performance in school. The dog's motivation is simpler: he enjoys sleeping on furniture because it is comfortable.

Pets living with single owners are not immune to triangulation. A third party does not have to be present to have an impact on the emotional processes within a dyad. For example, a young woman in her 20s is living alone and adopts a puppy for companionship. Her parents call (from 3,000 miles away) to criticize her handling of the puppy. The young woman might feed her parents information about a "naughty" puppy that confirms their view that the daughter could not get by without their advice. On the other hand, the daughter keeps her parents engaged. She might reject her parent's advice and do the opposite of what they suggest. Consequently, she ends up rejecting even useful advice. If the behavior consultant comes in with similar advice, without first earning the right to lead, the daughter will reject that as well, due to the triangulation occurring in the system.

Coalitions

A spouse may form a coalition with an animal, against or to the exclusion of her significant other. It is a familiar scene: The wife (usually) is tightly bonded with the dog and the dog becomes intent on "protecting" her, his precious resource, from the husband. The excluded party, the husband, supports this pattern by keeping his distance.

Who caused this problem? Chances are the dog has inherent tendencies to guard, but the problem is perpetuated and maybe even escalated because his guarding meets the emotional needs of his owners. Typically, the husband grumbles that the dog is coming between him and his wife, but unconsciously he may feel relieved that the dog is filling in for him and thus sparing him responsibility for working on the marriage.

An owner might form a coalition with the dog against outsiders. I know of a dog who will not let anyone near his elderly owner; they are a "good enough" team because the woman does not care much for socializing. She is afraid of people. Does the dog sense his owner's vulnerability and fearfulness, feel afraid, and take matters into his own paws? We all know of dog owners with phobias (irrational fears) whose dogs also appear to develop magnified fearfulness. These dogs might exhibit better behavior in a home with a strong leader with whom the dog feels safe and protected. I have facilitated rehoming for a number of Toy dogs who had bitten in prior homes where their needs for security were not being met and the emotional forces were arrayed against them. These Toys became excellent companions in new homes where the leadership was strong and nurturing. In good-enough relationships, dogs look to their humans to determine whether they are safe or not.

If you work for a shelter, I hope that you do not rely solely on temperament testing to determine if there is a future for dogs in your care. The question for evaluators ought to be, could the dog function adequately if given the benefit of a healthy relationship? Some dogs do an about-face almost immediately when they are in *right relationships* with good-enough families.

Regulating tension

In another type of arrangement, triangulated family members assume the role of go-between for others, thus balancing loyalties and regulating tension and intimacy. As a behavior consultant, how often have you felt called upon to serve as a go-between for couples? You might help them regulate tensions by deferring first to one, then to the other. Perhaps a husband is intent on showing you that the wife is somewhat inept, the evidence being that their dog is not housetrained. The husband does not mention that he habitually ignores signs that the dog needs to eliminate—in other words, he is not giving either the dog or his wife the support they need. You are supposed to fix the problem, but without the husband's support.

Families triangulate according to the level of tension in the system and as a measure of how much tension they can tolerate. When the tension level is mild to moderate, the conflict may be contained within one central triangle. One example of this is a father-mother-child triad. This can be seen is some father-mother-child stable triangles. However, if the levels of tension increase beyond the system's capacity to adapt, things get complicated. Members may create adjoining or interlocking triangles that involve other people or animals.

The following example illustrates how tensions shift through interlocking triangles: A father and mother were stressed by their adolescent son's push for autonomy. When the conflict became particularly intense, the father ensnared the dog by insisting that the teenager walk the dog at inconvenient times. The son became angry at the dog; this "safe" response left the original father-mother-dog triangle relatively stable. However, the dog, stressed by the teenager's rough treatment, developed elimination problems. The family called in a trainer, who blamed the teenager. The teenager and the trainer were then in conflict over the dog, and the father-mother-son triangle remained stable. The trainer met a need for the family, but did not help the dog. To help dogs, consultants generally have to forego blame altogether. Blame is akin to positive punishment: It drives problems underground and, inevitably, meets with walls of resistance.

When you are working with families and there is a good bit of tension and emotional reactivity, a good rule of thumb is, "don't rock the boat." Detach. Be factual. Tell stories about dogs with similar problems that were successfully resolved. Keep your focus on problem solving. There surely are situations that call for a passionate response but it is generally better to err on the side of blandness than reactivity to reactive systems.

Splitting

In cases where you, as the professional, are the third leg of a dysfunctional triangle, watch for evidence of *splitting*. That is, families may unite against you, another professional, or a rescue organization or healthcare provider. This pattern needs to be distinguished from normal situations of despair, such as when a family must relinquish a pet or turn him over for euthanasia. Expect that a number of families will get angry while they work their way through grief and suffering. Some venting is both normal and therapeutic.

If you detect splitting, pull back so that when you do move ahead, you are as independent of the system as possible and can disengage from family conflict.

The Role of Anxiety in Triangulation

Why do some families and other systems manage to work through their issues in straightforward ways, while others resort to triangulation that may result in significant dysfunction? According to psychiatrist Murray Bowen, the father of family systems theory, the higher the *level of anxiety* in a system, the greater the propensity to triangulate. Bowen likened the action in families to the movement of heated molecules. Anxiety is the "heat" that increases the activity of triangles.[1]

---

[1] Kerr, Michael, M.D., (1981) "Family Systems Theory and Therapy" in *Handbook of Family Therapy*, edited by A. Gurman and D. Kniskern. Brunner/Mazel: New York. p. 241

If you do not understand Bowen's point, consider it this way: *Why is anxiety the "heat" that increases the activity of triangles, simulating the movement of bouncing heated molecules?* To get at the truth of Bowen's statement about the effects of anxiety in systems, keep an eye on your own problem solving activities and the level of anxiety in your family when you attempt to negotiate issues. When are you at the peak of competence? When do you feel off-balance, diminished in your ability to address problems in an objective, straightforward way? Let us suppose you are extremely busy and your mother calls. While you are on the phone with her, she figures out that you are also typing. She could say, "I must have caught you at a bad time, why don't I call back later? I will let you get your work done." Your mother's response does not cause you to feel anxious. You respond, "No, I'll have even less time later and besides, I'm really interested and I can multitask" or, "How about if I call you in a few days when I'm finished with my project?" You and your mother resolve the problem without becoming emotional.

On the other hand, what if your mother calls and hears you typing and she asks, "Are you typing?" and you say, "Yes, I am swamped with work." She responds with a long silence that seems to convey that you are doing something wrong by not giving her your full attention. She says, "I'm sorry I bothered you" and quickly gets off the phone. You feel anxious, guilty because you disappointed your mother, and angry with her for being insensitive to your needs. You then have difficulty returning to your work and worry that she will complain to your father and siblings that you are rude and thoughtless. In short, your mother turned up the thermostat, got the "molecules" bouncing, and, as a result, you became more anxious and less productive.

Insiders and outsiders

In triangles, there are typically two insiders and one outsider. Would you rather be on the inside or the outside of a triangle? Here is what the family systems experts have to say about that: During periods of mild or moderate anxiety, the outsiders will long to belong and regret being isolated. However, when tensions are heightened, it is usually preferable to be on the outside and free from the tension of anxious, conflicted "players."[2]

Dog behavior professionals can bring family members who are outsiders inside to participate in problem solving.

Emotionality is the driving force

Bowen tells us that the key to understanding triangles is to recognize that emotionality drives them. The greater the togetherness orientation of the people, the greater the potential for anxiety and triangulation. Many issues are bandied about in triangles, but the *issues* are not the driving force. Rather, the process is driven by the *emotional reactivity* of participants and the level of emotion that they attach to particular issues. Reduction of anxiety and emotional reactivity will reduce the activity of triangles, but the basic pathways remain intact for future use.[3]

---

[2] Guerin, Philip, Thomas Fogarty, Leo Fay, and Judith Kautto (1996) *Working with Relationship Triangles: The One-Two-Three of Psychotherapy.* The Guilford, Press: New York. p. 67-69
[3] Kerr, Michael, M.D., (1981) "Family Systems Theory and Therapy", pg. 247 in *Handbook of Family Therapy,* edited by A. Gurman and D. Kniskern. Brunner/Mazel: New York. p. 241-242

Bowen posits that a strong leader maintains a non-anxious presence. An anxious, emotional system is a stressed system with diminished problem solving capabilities. This theme will be developed more fully in chapter six on the person of the animal behavior consultant.

Elimination problems

Indoor elimination problems really get the molecules hopping among family members who, if they have not given up, spend a percentage of their time anxiously tracking the whereabouts of the offending dog. Some members opt out by rejecting their dog. I will speculate that adolescents and men are most apt to withdraw from problem solving for dogs who eliminate in the home. When teenaged boys are asked to write essays for school, their topic will be the dog they are forced to live with and the misery the dog brings to their lives. Perhaps the husbands go off to work longing for the days when women were more proficient as housekeepers or dogs lived in the great outdoors.

Behavior consultants are apt to view dogs who eliminate indoors as incompletely housetrained (after medical causes have been ruled out) and we encourage families to go back to the beginning by using crates, tethering, regular visits outside, and reinforcement for eliminating in areas that humans consider appropriate. In addition, we ask owners to thoroughly clean and deodorize indoor spots so their dogs will not be drawn to them again.

Clients have often punished their dogs for "eliminating" in non-human sanctioned spots. I will ask, "Did punishment work?" In one form or another, the answer is always the same: punishment spawns anxiety and fear and worried dogs eliminate more, not less, and still do not know where to go. If dogs are eliminating in out-of-the way areas, such as living rooms or spare bedrooms, I also recommend that families change familiar patterns to communicate with their dogs about the true purpose of the areas the dogs have selected. That is, I suggest that families spend time in the off-the-beaten-path rooms. They can read in formal living rooms, sleep in spare bedrooms, and walk over the areas every day so they are fresh with human scent. In addition, the owners can put small training treats in the non-human sanctioned spots where their dog has been making his mistakes.

The function of rejection

It is worth noting that, according to family systems theorists (Bowen, Kerr), one of the most common mechanisms for maintaining equilibrium in a relationship system is rejection, and it is usually two against one or one group against another group. Rejection is a constant driving force between people—although they will rarely admit it. Interestingly, the family systems theorists report that the ones who complain that they have been rejected are usually doing the rejecting.

Dog behavior consultants should take note of triangulation among colleagues that may include rejection. For example, a practitioner may leave a professional group and tell others that she was not wanted by the group when the truth is that the supposed "victim" was unable or unwilling to work through issues and find a satisfactory way to belong, so that, long before she would have been rejected, she quit. Nevertheless, in the retelling, the group rejected her. Similarly, client families may tell you they were rejected by a veterinary practice—and perhaps they were!—but it may be you who will be next in their line of fire. That is, the family might reject you but say you rejected or somehow failed to care for them.

Rejection by rescue workers

Rescue workers also are in a position to triangulate and reject. In its most virulent form, a rescue worker might have a falling out with a prospective adoptive family, conclude that the family is unsuitable, and pass the "bad owner" label along to other rescue groups in the area. If other rescuers join in, the family may be effectively blacklisted from adopting an animal. Perhaps the family should not have a dog, but careful questioning might reveal that the family is being scapegoated by a rescue worker with limited interpersonal skills, over non-essential issues.

We would probably all agree that dogs are better served by individuals who have learned to negotiate issues without letting things become personal. It is true that some families will not provide good homes for dogs, but the situation is what it is and can be dealt with objectively, without emotionality and blame.

Rescue workers triangulate in other ways that are not good for animals. We all know that malevolent people do try to adopt dogs, and the workers have to screen potential adopters to protect dogs from abuse and exploitation. Dysfunction occurs when rescue workers apply the same level of scrutiny to good families who just want a dog. A rescue worker might call veterinarians or others who have had contact with the family, without permission, and possibly reveal confidential information. They may take suspicions to an internet list and repeat potentially damaging information there. Alternatively, the rescue worker might show too many personal biases. The family then decides the worker cannot be trusted. If they like the dog and adopt anyway, but have problems with him later, there is not a good foundation for the family to come back to the group for support or to trust the shelter to refer competently. We might suspect that families who discover post-adoption that their dog has issues will more likely return their dogs to shelters whose staffs have not shown an ability to work through problems professionally, in a way that inspires trust. We would have to research this sequence to know for sure.

All family members have contributed somewhat equally to the process

We have established here that individuals cannot be understood outside the context of their families. Similarly, no relationship can be understood outside of the context of how each relationship interlocks with other family relationships. For example, we may admire the calm or harmony of a couple's relationship. If we look further, we may realize that harmony is maintained only because there is conflict in another significant relationship, perhaps with a child, a dog, or the family-of-origin. We do encounter families whose relationships are nurturing and their stability is not achieved at the expense of others.

Chronic disorders in families

Is there an illness in a family whose struggles for control are ongoing? An illness can help the affected member gain the upper hand. For instance, in a couple with long-standing conflicts related to gender roles, a wife may refer to her chronic back pain to legitimize asking her spouse to do more of the housework—and the dog care.

Assessment and emotionality

We are emotional beings and how we feel provides clues that help us understand situations, but we need to get beyond emotional pulls to assess reliably. That is, while our feelings serve as reliable diagnostic indicators that help us figure out what is going on in systems, intellect and objectivity are the vehicles that carry us to the deeper truths.

For example, when clients or colleagues do not agree with you on an issue, do you continue to hold them and yourself in high regard and go on your way? Alternatively, do you feel hurt and worry that they do not like you, then progress to not liking them either? Or do you observe them objectively over time to discern if they simply have a different point of view on the one issue but will likely join with you later on different issues? If you feel yourself being bounced around by emotional forces, think of Bowen's heated molecules and what you can do to calm yourself so you can assess reliably.

Summary

In sum, when families are resistant to change or are not changing in the direction of their goals and you can find no reasonable explanation, suspect triangulation. If you perceive that you are being pulled in or pushed against, suspect triangulation.

As noted previously, triangulation can involve social systems that may include animals, veterinary office staff, groomers, rescue organizations, and of course, behavior consultants. These systems, in turn, have triangles of their own that involve families and can either help or impinge on the welfare of dogs.

Dog professionals create their own intense triangles when they position themselves as rescuers of "misunderstood" dogs. Unless the professional is intent on taking a dog home as a way of improving his life, and the family is willing to relinquish ownership, our best and only option is to draw families and other service providers in, rather than work against them.

Finally, emotional reactivity creates anxiety and increases the activity of triangles. ∎

Chapter 4

THE FAMILY

LIFECYCLE

Families go through developmental stages. Each stage brings fresh demands that force family members to accommodate to new needs. Families show varying degrees of resistance to change. They tend to gravitate to the familiar. However, to survive and thrive, families have to "change with change."

What of the families who cannot change? Perhaps a primary breadwinner's job is at risk but the family fails to read the signs of the times. They are in denial and they hold on when they should be letting go. The axe falls long before the breadwinner has started a search for a new job. As a result, he weakens his position and suffers a longer period of unemployment.

Families do suffer when they hold on to old ways and do not adapt to new challenges. What if a parent develops a serious illness and the family fails to reorganize to meet new demands? What if a family adopts a puppy and refuses to puppy-proof their home? Rather, they want to continue as it was pre-puppy and the puppy is expected to adapt to an old regimen. In another scenario, the family may long for a dog who died and refuse to re-orient themselves to the needs of a new dog, who then, lacking appropriate guidance, fails to "measure up." The dog behavior consultant is in a strong position to awaken families to new responsibilities and assist them in moving along the developmental continuum.

In our role as diagnosticians, we need to consider all factors that have an impact on dogs, including life issues in families. We may need to ask ourselves, for example:

> ➤ At what stage of the family lifecycle is the family? What are their major issues?

> ➤ Are we dealing with a family in transition? That is, did the family recently move? Was there a major job change? Is there a new baby and the dog is showing signs of being unprepared? Did grown children recently leave home? Did anyone marry or divorce?

> ➤ What competing obligations does the family have?

> ➤ Is this a family with a ghost? That is, do they have unresolved issues over the loss of a family member or companion animal that are being played out in the present?

> ➤ Are they struggling with major illnesses?

> ➤ What other changes are there that might affect the dog's relationships and familiar patterns?

Our understanding of families in different phases of the lifecycle provides wellsprings of hope for dogs. Compassionate understanding helps us identify, for example, why a dog might not do well in one home but is likely to thrive in another. Decisions to rehome are difficult, but transitions are eased when we correctly identify under what circumstances dogs might make a satisfactory adjustment. Sometimes all a dog needs to succeed is a family in a more compatible phase of life.

If we are alert to what is going on in client families, just as we are watchful for cues to what is going on with dogs, we will more likely connect with families appropriately (a family can be a single adult) and suggest interventions that can be carried out successfully. This principle holds true as you work with families at various stages in the lifecycle. To bring the point home, would your assessment be the same and would you recommend the same interventions for a 10-week-old puppy and a 10-year-old dog with the same problems? Of course, you would not. The puppy and dog are at different stages of development.

If you do not have experience with a phase—that is, you are not there yet—know that you may not have the best understanding of what a family needs from you and what they should do. Solutions have to work for both dogs and owners. Humility dictates that we let families educate us about their issues. If you are working with a family that has a child with a disability, for example, do not assume that you know what the right balance is between care for the child and attention to a dog. Provide some options and let the family show you which interventions are workable and which will add unwelcome stress.

For the rest of this section, please refer to the family lifecycle chart in the pages that follow. Dr. Monica McGoldrick, esteemed author and family therapist from Highland Park, New Jersey, created the conceptual schematic that follows to help us understand family struggles during different developmental stages.[1]

---

[1] Monica McGoldrick, The Multicultural Family Institute. *Web: www.multiculturalfamily.org*

Family Lifecycle Stage	Emotional Process of Transition: Key Principles	Second-order Changes in Family Status Required to Proceed Developmentally
1. Leaving home: Single young adults	Accepting emotional and financial responsibility for self	a. Differentiation of self in relation to family of origin b. Development of intimate peer relationships c. Establishment of self in relation to work and financial independence
2. The joining of families through marriage: The new couple	Commitment to new system	a. Formation of marital system b. Realignment of relation-ships with extended families and friends to include spouse
3. Families with young children	Accepting new members into the system	a. Adjusting marital system to make space for child(ren) b. Joining in child-rearing, financial, and household tasks c. Realignment of relation-ships with extended family to include parenting and grandparenting roles
4. Families with adolescents	Increasing flexibility of family boundaries to include children's independence and	a. Shifting of parent-child relationships to permit adolescents to move in and out of system b. Refocus on mid-life marital and career issues

	grandparents' frailties	c. Beginning shift toward joint caring for older generation
5. Launching children and moving on	Accepting the shifting of generational roles	a. Renegotiation of marital system as a dyad b. Development of adult-to-adult relationships c. Realignment of relationships to include in-laws and grandchildren
6. Families in later life		a. Maintaining own and/or couple functioning and interests in face of physiological decline; exploration of new familial and social-role options b. Support for a more central role of middle generation c. Making room in the system for the wisdom and experience of the elderly; supporting the older generation without over-functioning for them d. Dealing with loss of spouse, siblings, and other peers and preparation for own death. Life review and integration.

Reprinted with permission, from Carter, Elizabeth and Monica McGoldrick, (eds.) (2004). *The changing family lifecycle: A framework for family therapy (4th Ed.).* Allyn and Bacon: Boston

Leaving Home:
The Single Young Adult
The first stage of the family lifecycle

Key emotional processes:
Accepting emotional and financial responsibility for self

Changes in family status required to proceed developmentally:
1. The differentiation of self in relation to family of origin
2. The development of intimate peer relationships
3. The establishment of self in relation to work and financial independence

The young adult is reaching out, seeking enjoyment, exploring and testing, and in search of mutual encounters. Young people just venturing forth from home may adopt a dog to ease the transition. With a dog, he or she is never alone. Perhaps the dog barks protectively and the owner feels safe. Sometimes the dog is so protective that he is not welcoming of outsiders, thereby isolating the owner. Conversely, the owner may be so busy that the dog is spending too much time alone. Alternatively, the owner might become involved in a relationship with someone who does not like dogs. The dog may be left out and develop behavior problems that result from the loss of owner attention. Dogs fare better when they are accepted as "part of the package"—just as enchanting as the owner is. If the significant other is not kind to the dog, that person, not the dog, may be left behind.

Sometimes dogs become the focal point of struggles for separation-individuation between young adult owners and their parents. The old theme of "we don't like your boyfriend (or girlfriend)" may be played out as "we don't like your dog," or, worse for the humans, "we like your dog but we don't like you."

Single young adults are frequently in transition, and dogs are routinely left behind when they do not fit in with new situations. For example, shelters in some college towns are known to fill up at the end of the school year when students return to their families of origin for the summer and their "best friends" are not welcome to come along.

Joining of Family Through Marriage: The Young Couple
The second stage of the family lifecycle

The key emotional process:
Commitment to the new system

Changes required to proceed developmentally:
1. Formation of the marital system
2. The realignment of relationships with extended families and friends to include the spouse

Young people head into the world with a knapsack full of values and beliefs carried across from their families of origin. Courtship begins with the high phase of mutual idealization and a focus on similarities. Nevertheless, conflict is inevitable and as you might expect, the two individuals, on their way to forming a more perfect union, eventually awaken to their differences. Each will have to relinquish some values along the way to meet the developmental challenges of merging two families into one. Some values that may be given up relate to dog's roles in families and families' responsibilities to dogs.

We all know that some ideas that are passed along through the generations about dogs cause harm to dogs and to dog-human relationships. Most families expect that their dogs will enhance rather than detract from family life. Families with rigid belief systems might not rise to the occasion when their dog is in need. *Dogs are routinely put to death for treatable health and behavior problems.* These actions are culturally acceptable. We take a risk if we demand that families take better care of their dogs. If they have to extend themselves too far, it is likely that fewer will open their homes to dogs. Nevertheless, dog behavior consultants have an obligation to try to influence familial and societal values as they pertain to dogs.

Let us stop to consider that there are many owners and trainers who believe that dogs who bite humans should be put to death. I remember all too well the young man who told me how much he adored a Shetland Sheepdog who had served as his closest companion for years. The dog was his best friend and saw him through a painful divorce. Yet, when the dog bit him, a level 2 bite to the hand, he had the dog euthanized. In his mind, euthanasia was a just end for a biting dog. Reportedly, his veterinarian did not question his decision. We will never know if the dog was ill or if the relationship was off-course but repairable. We do know that this man believed euthanasia was the correct and only option!

As dog behavior consultants, we are in a unique position to help couples improve upon generational patterns that affect dogs. This stage of life is perhaps the most opportune time because young couples are transitioning to new values anyway. We can influence both how the new family unit interacts with their dogs and what ideas will be passed along to future generations. In later stages of family life, the resistance to change might be stronger because members are busy defending the values they have selected.

Many newly married couples I encounter pour a lot of energy into raising their dog. These couples often plan to raise children together and may feel that their competence as future parents is being tested. That is, if they do a good job of raising their dog, they gain confidence in themselves as nurturers of children. To illustrate, I worked with a young couple who dropped their pup off at daycare and were dismayed and more than a little offended when the daycare staff let them know their dog was a problem. "Daycare says he's 'over the top.' Do you think he's over the top?" they asked, sounding wounded. I see a similar hurt response in parents whose preschoolers are banished from nursery school or daycare because of hyperactivity.

It is so important to some young couples to "turn out" behaviorally healthy animals, that when things go wrong, it is this age group that will most likely ask, "Did we cause this?" Indeed, a young couple may have "performance anxiety" and transmit this anxiety to their puppy, who then develops behavior problems. In one study, 81% of participants reported that their pets have developed seizures and gastrointestinal symptoms in response to anxiety and tension with their families.[1]

---

[1] Cain, A.O. (1983) A study of pets in the family system. In *New Perspectives on Our Lives with Companion Animals,* ed. A.H. Katcher and A.M. Beck. University of Pennsylvania Press: Philadelphia. p. 72-81

The primary goal in working with these families is to help them develop competencies so they are successful at raising their puppy or dog. Focus on their strengths. Let them know that you regard them as capable caregivers. It is easy to imagine that families cause behavior problems in dogs, even in dogs who were recently adopted or rescued post-puppyhood. Do not get too carried away. It is hard to think of anyone who benefits when we point fingers of blame. Dogs are born with certain tendencies for trouble. The owners who worry, "Are we causing our dog's problems?" might be competent, and the dog might be in worse shape without their loving guidance and protection.

I trained as a family therapist in the 1970s, and at the time we were taught that families, especially mothers, caused mental illness. Today we know better. We have sophisticated diagnostic imaging tools and a body of research to show us without a doubt that there are strong hereditary components and biological processes at work in disorders such as bipolar (also known as manic-depressive illness), autism, schizophrenia, anxiety, phobias, and others. Imagine how hurtful it must have been for the parents of mentally ill children when professionals who were supposed to know the truth blamed them! We need to be part of the solution and not make ourselves part of the problem. Similarly, we should be concerned with how to dislodge problems, not who caused them. It behooves us to organize our thinking about dogs so there are solutions, not so we have opportunities to blame.

Moving on, young couples who love their dogs and want to have babies together have different worries. If their dog has "issues," they know that she might not hold up for the next phase of life with young children.

Indeed, some dogs do have traits that make adaptation to a baby difficult or unlikely. For example, the serious resource guarder will very likely aggress against approaching toddlers. Milder tendencies to aggress and protect can sometimes be overcome by a combination of management and behavior modification.

Like it or not, children usually rank ahead of dogs in family hierarchies. If an at-risk dog is young and can be rehomed successfully now, but not if you wait a few years, you might suggest rehoming the dog sooner rather than later, while the dog is still adoptable.

Consultants offer motivated couples lifelong management strategies and training plans so that problematic behaviors can be modified and controlled. You might consider offering sessions aimed at helping dogs of expectant families adapt to babies and children. As noted, young couples are looking for *empowerment*. In contrast, later-stage families may be content to sit back and let us do the work of bringing about change in their dogs.

It is important to note that couple arrangements do not have to be legal to be significant. We encounter the same themes among homosexual couples and unmarried couples living together as we do with conventionally married couples.

Families with Young Children
The third stage of the family lifecycle

The key emotional process:
Accepting new members into the system

Changes required to proceed developmentally:
1. Adjusting the marital system to make space for child(ren)
2. Joining in child-rearing, financial, and household tasks
3. The realignment of relationships with extended family to include parenting and grandparenting roles

The arrival of a baby profoundly changes relationships on all fronts. Before the baby, husbands and wives have each other to turn to for mutual nourishment. Now, they must turn their attention to a helpless and dependent infant whose needs come first.

The mother may take prime responsibility for the infant, with the father supporting and nurturing the mother as she does so. Or, they may share care more equally. Whatever the arrangement, they lose each other's exclusive attention and typically have less time and energy for a dog. Dogs stand to lose more than they gain during this phase. Gone are the delightful romps in the park or lying contentedly on a sofa, head resting on an owner's lap. If the dog fails to adapt to life with a baby, the dog is the "weaker link" and will likely be left behind.

Some dogs who co-exist peacefully with babies are less enamored of mobile toddlers who touch the dog's toys, approach food dishes, and plop down on favored sleeping spots. Even dogs who bond with children in their own families may not be as welcoming of friends' children. Moreover, dogs who bite children are not well tolerated in most homes.

Many dogs do adapt, however. Indeed, babies in highchairs who drop food provide positive reinforcement that shores up many dog-baby relationships. Some dogs find added satisfaction in protecting *their* baby, but run into trouble if they are unable to set guarding behavior aside for visitors, such as extended family who rarely visit and bear a curious resemblance to strangers.

If a dog is protective and a father travels, the dog's desire to guard may prove an asset to the family. However, sometimes fear aggression surfaces when a spouse hits the road, leaving the mother—and, apparently, the dog—feeling vulnerable. When one spouse is gone, the remaining spouse must take on additional nurturing and leadership functions, or the children and dog may have to make do with less.

Families must grow into and then outgrow each stage. The question becomes, can their dogs grow with them?

One study found that "households with children at home tended to have more pets than either widows or families with an 'empty nest', or with an infant. However, feelings of attachment to the pet were lowest in families where children were at home."[2]

Dogs who bite children are especially at risk of losing their homes and even their lives. For example, a family with young children had a 9-month-old Maltese who recently started growling at and biting (no puncture) their elementary-school aged children. After the second incident, the family called a trainer, who recommended by phone that the dog be euthanized. Our professional association, the International Association of Animal Behavior Consultants (IAABC), takes a stand against members recommending euthanasia for animals who have not had the benefit of a professional evaluation. The IAABC Code of Ethics mandates an evaluation, partially because experience has shown that many dogs can be rehomed successfully. Their biting is contextual, specific to the environment.

On the positive side, dogs provide the most wonderful companionship and many survive and thrive with babies and growing children. What is childhood without a dog? I remember when we bought our children a Labrador Retriever puppy, Andy, to ease their transition to a new city. He was the rock who saw them through our moves and the difficulties of adolescence.

---

[2] Albert, A. and K. Bulcroft (1988). *Pets, families, and the life course.* Journal of Marriage and Family Therapy, 50. p. 543-52. In Serpell, James. (2003) *The Domestic Dog.* p. 165.

He was always there when they returned home with stubbed toes, hurt feelings, or a wish to hug or share an apple. Because of Andy, our children were never home alone. He contributed immeasurably to their development and sense of security and well-being.

Families with Adolescents
The fourth stage of the family lifecycle

The key emotional process:

Increasing the flexibility of family boundaries to include growing children's independence and grandparents' frailties

Changes required to proceed developmentally:
1. The shifting of parent-child relationships to permit adolescents to move in and out of the system
2. A refocus on mid-life marital and career issues
3. A beginning shift toward joint caring for the older generation

While teenagers push for autonomy, the parents have a reciprocal responsibility to let go, but not too much. They must be tuned in, but not overly so. A dog in the home helps families achieve a right balance. Dogs who might not fare well in other phases of the family lifecycle could succeed during this phase.

A dog serves as a transitional object for parents when they dote on the dog instead of their growing children. A good dog often serves as a counselor who consoles. Our Labrador is the charming fellow whom our teens' friends stop by to visit, because time with Andy heals wounds. He is invited to their parties and serves as official vacuum cleaner and best friend to anyone with pizza! It is important for teenagers to feel accepted, and he loves them all. He is great fun on a hike. He growls at strangers (and strange cats) if they are lurking about . . . or just strolling by.

On the other hand, we also have a  Yorkshire Terrier, Piper, who is intensely devoted to me. I tend to him like a baby, and my children are relieved that this attention is heaped on Piper and not them! As young adults, they have a wider world to explore and my Yorkie tempers any tendency I might have to overprotect.

It must be noted that couples are having children later in life and may be sandwiched between their growing children's need and those of aging parents in declining health. In this situation, the dog may suffer from loss of attention. On the other hand, research shows that caregivers are less likely to burn out if they have a dog as a companion for the journey.

Families of divorce face different struggles, and dogs are frequently drawn into combat between warring parents. If there are no children to fight over, the separating parties might fight over a dog instead. On the flip side, it is often a beloved dog who sees children through upheavals in parental subsystems. 'Tis a cruel fate when children lose their dogs to divorce.

Divorce is more damaging to children than we like to think. Research shows that no matter how well divorce is handled, children need intact families and they suffer developmentally when parents separate.[3]

With *stepfamilies*, it is important to keep in mind that new families begin after many losses and changes. Moreover, members' "knapsacks" are filled with rules carried over from previous households. One of the stepfamily's primary tasks is to establish *new rules* and *new traditions* so that couples develop strong bonds and new relationships are formed. This is a time of transition, and specifically, transition to new values. Behavior that was tolerated in an old home may be "beyond the limits" in a new home. Children typically have to adapt to different rules for each home. Changes to the rules and traditions also have an impact on dogs, for better or worse.

In addition, families have to adjust to continual shifts in household composition. The children in blended families may be in different developmental stages and have unique needs that may or may not be met by blended families.

It takes a tremendous amount of energy for stepfamilies to successfully make the transition and achieve balance. I have worked with stepfamilies who were sensitively tuned in to their dog's needs but ignored

---

[3] Wallerstein, Judith, Julia Lewis and Sandra Blakeslee (2000) *The Unexpected Legacy of Divorce: A 25 Year Landmark Study.* Hyperion: New York

the plight of their children; one family expected the children to tiptoe around an aggressive dog. Nevertheless, dogs are generally much more at-risk than children are during this and all phases of family life.

Launching Children and Moving On
The fifth stage of the family lifecycle

The key emotional process:
Accepting the shifting of generational roles

Changes required to proceed developmentally:
1. Renegotiation of the marital system as a dyad, or twosome
2. The development of adult-to-adult relationships
3. The realignment of relationships to include in-laws and grandchildren

The original family is once again a family of two. This "empty nest" phase can be as rich as any other, if the partners, while building careers and raising children, have also developed their individuality as separate persons as well as developing their relationship. Indeed, they may realize possibilities that were unattainable when they were preoccupied with meeting their children's needs. However, dogs may suffer when the children leave home, unless remaining family members fill the void.

Dogs can hold a special place in the hearts of families whose children leave home. When George W. and Laura Bush's English Springer Spaniel, Spot, died, the White House issued this statement, reported by the Associated Press: "All the family is deeply saddened by Spot's passing. Spot was a beloved member of the Bush family for nearly 15 years. She will be missed. Mrs. Bush has often said that—*especially with the Bush's two daughters away at college*—talking about and playing with the dogs and the family's cat, Willy, are a large part of the couple's entertainment."[4]

Be alert to families with a *ghost*

The family with a ghost might say, "If my father were here, he would know what to do." Alternatively, the ghost might be a dog who died and the owner compares the present dog unfavorably with the dog they lost.

At this point you might ask, "So what if this is a family with a ghost? I can't bring back loved ones." To illustrate, I had a client with two members who were physically absent but very much alive in her mind: a deceased mother and a deceased German Shepherd whom my client, the daughter, described as "the perfect dog." This middle-aged woman who was living alone with an adolescent, male German Shepherd called me because the dog was afraid (thunderstorms, sudden movement, noise, strangers) and had started barking and lunging at passing dogs and people while

---

[4] CNN.COM. U.S. News Report. Saturday, February 21, 2004. *Spot, spaniel born in first Bush White House, dies.*

out for walks on leash. The owner let me know that her mother used to breed German Shepherds and had been her daughter's advisor on all dog-related matters until she died a year ago. She was apprehensive about calling me and regretted that her mother was not available to serve as her consultant. She acutely missed both her mother and the dog who died a few months ahead of the mother.

The daughter was grieving for her mother and dog. She hoped that I would give her a satisfying emotional experience, similar to what she could count on when her mother served as the "dog expert." I considered that she might also want me to make her current "replacement" dog more like the dog she lost (instead of the dog he was).

During the home visit, I paused to look at family pictures that served as décor for the room. The mother struck me as a stern, no-nonsense, take-charge type of person with a nurturing, caretaking side to her. This was confirmed by the daughter's descriptions of her. I noted that all the dogs in the pictures wore choke collars. Therefore, I started asking questions about dogs in the family and interspersed these with the question, "What would your mother say you should do?" Of course, the mother's ideas were outdated, calling for harsh verbal corrections and choke chains with leash pops to teach loose-leash walking and inhibit lunging.

Animal behavior consultants are ethically bound (see the IAABC Code of Ethics and Practice Guidelines) to search for the least intrusive and minimally aversive methods to modify, train and manage behaviors. The mother's methods were more aversive than was necessary and worked against building the dog's confidence.

The challenge for me, as I understood it, was to be like the mother in style when I presented new information about dogs. That is, I set out to introduce "softer" strategies in a gruff, no-nonsense way. As such, I took command of the room and left no space for questioning; I moved in quickly to demonstrate modern training techniques.

German Shepherds are used as police dogs. They are trained for protection and go off to war. We might speculate that some owners of German Shepherds are attracted to the breed because of their perceived power and protective tendencies. They are often pictured in choke collars and owners are drawn to this training tool as well, as a symbol of power and prestige. In other words, it can be difficult to wean them away from choke collars because they have a nostalgic attachment to them.

With this client, therefore, I introduced less aversive tools but used "power" terms to describe them. I could have said, "I do not believe in choke collars," but that would be fighting the ghost of the mother. The daughter would have decided I was a sorry substitute for her mother and we would not have accomplished our goals for the session. So instead, I talked about the breed's long history with choke collars without a hint of disapproval, but went on to describe the new and more "powerful" tools on the market that are even more effective, incredible in their simplicity, even handsome, such as a properly fitted Premier Easy Walk harness. This way, the daughter could be faithful to her mother and yet adopt modern methods.

We also had to deal with the daughter's disappointment over having a "soft" German Shepherd. She wanted a dog who gave her confidence. The problem was that both dog and daughter needed the same thing: Confident leadership. They were not well matched. Nevertheless, the daughter ultimately did step in to her mother's shoes just enough to work the dog away from his leash aggression and other problems.

Families in Later Life
The sixth stage of the family lifecycle

Changes required to proceed developmentally:
1. Maintaining one's own and/or couple functioning and interests in the face of physiological decline; exploration of new familial and social-role options
2. Support of a more central role for the middle generation
3. Making room in the system for the wisdom and experience of the elderly; supporting the older generation without over-functioning for them
4. Dealing with the loss of a spouse, siblings, and other peers and preparation for one's own death; life review and integration

Elderly people are more alone today than ever, and a dog can make an amazing difference during the years of loss and declining health. The final years can be rich, especially if the aging grow in their love for people, animals, and causes outside themselves. The less attractive alternative would be a narrow preoccupation with self. The dog behavior consultant who is well informed about the health benefits of dogs has more to bring to families during this stage.

If you are in a position to influence the choice of dogs, keep in mind that safety issues are paramount. The elderly have slower response times and they do not recover as quickly from physical trauma.

I worked with an older couple whose grown children had given them a Doberman Pinscher puppy as a gift. They were living in a neighborhood that was not as safe as it once was, but they both were rooted to the area and did not want to move. Their children, fishing for solutions, hoped a Doberman would provide some protection. However, as the puppy grew in size and exuberance, she became a threat to the aging parents' health, perhaps more so than the neighborhood. For example, when the pup was six months old, she slammed into the wife in yet another grab for her hair and the wife ended up in a hospital emergency room for stitches to repair a deep gash to her forehead. The story has a happy outcome because the couple were determined that they would train the dog no matter what, though training was a challenge because the puppy was quick and opportunistic, whereas they were slow. Nevertheless, they persisted and prevailed, and due to their goodness, the dog still has her home. In fact, because of her exuberant and undimmed zest for life, the dog is a joy to the couple. ■

Chapter 5
INFLUENCING CHANGE

As we embark on our mission to help dogs, we must embrace our responsibilities to the families who care for them. We want families to change how they interact with their dogs, but the path to change is seldom straightforward. Families are systems and systems are lulled by homeostasis, or sameness, and defend against change.

For the purposes of our discussion, I will refer to families who have difficulty working their way through issues as dysfunctional. We all have areas of dysfunction, and behavior consultants can easily become partners to disarray in client families. The key is *not* to label families or ourselves; rather, we might suspect that family systems are dysfunctioning when they resist change to the degree that they are not able to resolve problems after being shown the way; success is within their grasp, but they do not embrace it.

As I have noted many times throughout this book, clients do not contract with us to evaluate family functioning or to try to change them. Nevertheless, the truth is that families become stuck and unless we get them moving in the direction of their goals, we will not be able to fulfill our contractual obligation to them and we will not help many dogs. In sum, we must know something about assessing and influencing change in families to do this.

The act of observation influences what is being observed

Our interactions with families and dogs influence how they interact with us; in turn, we are influenced by them. As such, we become part of the phenomenon being observed, "actors" in the play. We should keep in mind that if the cast of characters was changed, we might present ourselves differently. Of course, some behaviors manifest themselves no matter what is going on in the environment. For example, some dogs growl at every human or dog who comes within 25 feet of them, without exception. Some families become testy when they are criticized for what they are doing, no matter how the feedback is delivered—although most families respond well to feedback that is presented skillfully and tailored to them.

Our assessments, at best, approximate the truth. If we are unable to facilitate movement in systems, it is worth reexamining our assumptions. Are our lights on? Have we figured out what the problem really is?[1] Or, have we organized our understanding of problems so that we cannot find solutions?

One couple called me when they were at a point of desperation. I was the last hope for a fearful Spaniel mix whom they had rescued from a shelter. The dog

[1] Gause, Donald and Gerald Weinberg (1992) *Are Your Lights On? How to Figure Out What the Problem Really Is.* Dorset House Publishing: New York

was bonded to the husband but afraid of the wife. The wife tried to get the dog to like her and was concerned because her interactions seemed to cause him even more distress, as demonstrated when he urinated and defecated in the home. The couple hired a trainer to come to the house. The trainer asked the owners to have the dog on a leash. The dog barked incessantly, apparently alarmed now by the presence of both the trainer and the wife. Early on, the trainer asked them to lock the dog in a distant room and he continued barking there. The trainer blamed the wife for the dog's worrisome behavior and advised her not to attempt to interact with him. The wife was guilt-ridden and frustrated that no matter what she did, the dog did not respond to her. The dog had already bitten a deliveryman and the installer of his electronic containment system (who reportedly did not warn them that reactive dog's symptoms could be exacerbated by shocks delivered during training.) In sum, it was doubtful that the dog could be rehomed. If they turned him in to a shelter, euthanasia would be the likely outcome.

I approached the situation knowing that I would be part of the occurrence as well as an observer. I was sure that I would not assign blame. This is, I planned to manipulate the structural arrangements (how I positioned myself in relation to the dog and couple; how the couple positioned themselves in relation to the dog) to elicit healthier, original responses from the dog. Here is how I did it, drawing from family systems constructs.

The husband had the dog on a leash with the dog trying to hide behind him. I discerned that the dog was not going to bite me, so I asked the husband to let him off the leash to give him the freedom to put himself at a comfortable distance from me (with fight or flight as choices, he would choose flight). I did not want the dog banished to another room so we could "get things done." Instead, I asked the wife to cook up a hot dog, adding a little olive oil and garlic powder. (When a dog is in danger of losing his home, I do not worry about good nutrition; I do *not* use fresh garlic, however. I had asked the family not to feed the dog before I arrived.) The aroma of slow-cooking hot dog naturally caught the attention of the hungry dog. Keeping my distance, I asked the wife to put the hot dog on a small plate and the four of us moved to an area in their dining room with the wife holding the fresh-cooked hot dog. The dog was most interested in the food the wife was carrying. He continued his worried surveillance of me, but something interesting happened: He adopted the wife as his "new best friend." When I moved a smidgen, he became alarmed and edged closer to her and her hot dog. He seemed to forget about the husband; instead, he started relating to the oft-feared wife as his protector.

This was a turning point for the couple: They could see that their dog's fear of the wife and preference of the husband was not personal; it was just a pattern for the pooch to attach himself to one person and worry about everyone else in the room. For the first time, the wife, knowing she was not causing the dog's problems, could let go of her guilt. She had not "ruined" the dog after all! Husband and wife could laugh about their "neurotic" dog . . . and move on. Free from guilt, they tackled the behavior modification and management plan with zest and shifted to loving him just the way he was.

This case had a successful outcome. The couple developed strategies for helping the dog cope, and the dog kept his home. After my visit, the dog showed more attachment to the wife, especially when the husband was not home. She cooked hot dogs on days when he seemed more apprehensive, so he would warm to her and not "advance" to eliminating in the home.

This family went extra miles to achieve a satisfactory outcome. We had discerned that the dog was more confident when he was around other confident dogs. So the couple actually adopted an older puppy, carefully selected and earmarked for the wife (we reinforced bonding to her). The new dog was not worried about "enemies" and naturally turned to the wife for protection. This seems to have encouraged the Spaniel to trust the wife. We relied on standard behavior modification and management techniques, but it was the alleviation of owner guilt and the introduction of a confident puppy that provided the bulk of the relief.

Making sense

At this point, we might muse that we have watched Hollywood trainers on television make comments about dogs that we know are not credible, and yet their dog owning fans seem to believe them. Keep in mind that television cameras are part of the event you and the participants are observing. For the rest of us, families will resist if they sense that our assessments do not ring true or our ideas about dogs are fanciful.

"If it's not broken, don't fix it"

Client's have their preferred explanations for why their dogs engage in certain behaviors. Some blame themselves and ask us to fix them (the family) so their dogs will be whole again; others want the focus to be on their dogs, in sometimes peculiar ways. We usually challenge their explanations and offer fresh perspectives. However, sometimes we may decide to leave well enough alone—that is, we accept distorted, at times nonsensical explanations because they do not get in the way of problem solving and they appear to make owners feel better. Why try to fix something if it is not broken?

The (real) blame game

It may appear that one member of the family is hampering progress while another is your ally, but remember that all members of systems participate in maintaining systems—including you! Your "ally" might support your efforts only to the extent that other family members are guaranteed to thwart them. The result is the same: No change occurs and the problem they hired you to help them with is unresolved.

It may also seem that a family is to blame for their dog's problems. The wife who shared her home with the Spaniel mix was initially so convinced that she was bad for the dog that she wanted him gone. He was urinating and defecating in their beautiful home, and that was bad enough, but her guilt was the only element she really could not handle. Accordingly, why would we add guilt to any pot?

Many years ago, I worked briefly with an elderly woman who had owned Airedales all of her adult life. Only her current dog had behavioral issues. She bought him from a breeder and on his first day in his new home, at the age of five months, he bit a relative, apparently while guarding her for himself. She reported this to the breeder, who said that it was the owner's fault because she was not handling him correctly. Nevertheless, the breeder guaranteed that he would improve with age. In good faith, the woman kept trying. He aggressed with everyone from the outset, and, of course, became more, not less people-aggressive over time. The owner's many calls to the breeder were met with "you are making him aggressive but he will get better on his own." Meanwhile, her family and neighbors stopped visiting. They were afraid of the dog. The dog did not just growl and sometimes bite. He growled and clamored to get at visitors non-stop. He could never be let off a leash with anyone except the owner, because he was always straining, and when he occasionally did get free, if he connected with a human he would bite.

When he reached 16 months, the woman finally realized that he was growing progressively worse, and was not going to improve. With a sad heart and support from her family, she had him euthanized. I was called in at the end when the family asked me to talk to the woman about her loss and help her find a new dog who did not have aggressive tendencies.

I am haunted by this dog on several levels. One, the woman told me that euthanasia had been most humane because if she had tried to rehome him, he would have "pined away" for her. I was confident that it would have taken the dog no more than a few hours to bond to a new "special someone," and he would have been just as protective and aggressive for a new owner—and just as much of a problem to everyone else. He would not have been thinking about her. But, I joined with her instead—"Yes, he would have missed you terribly"—and this helped her as she grieved the loss of one dog and prepared herself to welcome a new one. This is an example of an instance when I decided not to try to fix what did not appear to be broken; the belief that he at least loved her desperately seemed to be helping her cope with the loss.

Second, could the outcome have been improved if the breeder had let the owner return the puppy when the problem first appeared? The dog might have had a chance with a strong leader who would have elicited better behaviors from the outset.

I considered that I possibly could have turned him around, but not with this owner.

Further, if the breeder had not assigned blame, the woman would not have tried for so long and she would not have suffered so much.

Finally, as it turned out, the breeder was hiding something from the owner: The "breeder" had actually rescued the dog from a puppy mill and almost immediately placed him with her. The puppy had been raised in a cage somewhere.

Ask yourself, who in the system is most committed to the dog's survival in the home?

Identify and cultivate relationships with the dog's apparent allies. However, do not set yourself against the opposition. Turn reluctant members into allies instead.

The value of feedback

Let families enlighten you if you are trying to move them in a wrong direction or do not understand the problem. Families are forgiving if we allow them to correct us.

Saving dogs?

Unless you plan to take the client's dog home with you and care for her forever—or you have a better home lined up for her and the client's permission to go off with their dog—the dog's best bet will be with the family she has. Try to find solutions that work *for* families, *within* families. I say this with a couple of caveats:

➤ Every so often, dogs genuinely need saving.

➤ Some dogs truly will do better in another home.

Joining

Joining is essential to any helping relationship. Joining means that we connect with people. That is, we find common ground, appreciate their values and life choices and speak languages that are meaningful to them.

Joining is "more of an attitude than a technique," according to Minuchin, author of *Family Therapy Techniques*. "Joining is the umbrella under which all other transactions occur. . . . joining is not a reasoned, deliberate process. Much of it occurs beneath the surface."[2] It lets the family know the dog behavior consultant understands them and is working with and for them. Joining is the glue that holds the alliance together. Under the dog behavior consultant's protec-

---

[2] Minuchin, Salvador and H. Charles Fishman (1990) *Family Therapy Techniques*. Harvard University Press: Cambridge. p. 31

tion and support, joining gives the family a sense of security while they explore alternatives. We have to join with families before they will let us lead.

Families call us in as experts, but we must earn the right to lead. Be prepared to sell yourself and know how to join with families so they will defer to you as a leader.

> ➤ Respect the family hierarchy. If family members turn to Grandma for advice on dogs, join with Grandma. Use similar terminology. Have a perspective that sounds somewhat the same. Listen respectfully to her opinions. Whatever you do, do not cast aspersions on Grandma's advice prematurely. Instead, win her support before changing directions.

> ➤ Pay attention to rules. Families have great power to induce us to function according to their rules. When you challenge family rules, expect that they will automatically be countered.

Some families fit us "like gloves," and we accommodate to them and they accommodate to us, naturally. It is an easy give and take and we think, "What nice people!" because we can be ourselves with them.

However, our natural styles are not as appreciated by all families. (*Style* is a non-technical term that refers to the way in which we express or carry ourselves.) In our role as helpers, we have an ethical obligation to stretch ourselves to communicate effectively with clients no matter what their style. Joining is one strategy we can use to help us influence families in positive ways. Thus, we could join by becoming more proper with families who are stiff and respond well to formality. We might become boisterous with loud families who respond well to big movements. We can become very quiet and introduce information peacefully to families who are easily "aroused" or are in an uproar. With other families, we become intense, direct, and hard-hitting to drive our points home.

Through our give and take with families, they shape our interactions with them. For example, what if a husband is easygoing and the wife seems intimidating? We might naturally drift toward the husband and try to work through him to help the dog. But, if we use ourselves effectively, in a purposeful, goal-directed way, we might succeed at connecting, or joining, with the wife, so her available energies can also be used for problem solving. When all is said and done, we may discover that the wife is the better ally. When the husband wants to give up, she sees the possibilities and is willing to work to keep the dog.

Story telling

We facilitate joining when we share stories about our own dogs. The stories must be relevant, and we learn not to reveal information that might disqualify us as experts. We tell stories in the hopes of moving families in the direction of their own goals, and not because we have a captive audience.

Have you ever found your clients listening intently to your "my dog" stories? Perhaps it helps them to size you up? In addition, they will learn quickly if there is a message in your story for them. If there is not something for them, the stories should not be told.

Goal-Directed Interventions

Of course, it is not enough to join with families. We have to help families achieve their goals. We need room to maneuver so that we can influence them. The strategy we use to join with families during the first session may not be the best choice for a later session. For example, we may decide during one session to ally with a dog who appears to be the family scapegoat. Later, we may join forces with a gruff family member whose assistance we need to help the dog. We choose tactics that are consistent with our goals.

How do we know what we have to work with in families? We are constantly assessing just as we continually assess the dogs in our care. Who turned the television on during your visit? When the husband and wife bickered, where did the dog plant himself?

To illustrate, a husband called me to help train his dog because the dog pulled on leash and bounced around the house. At the first session, he admitted to me that a mail carrier indicated that the dog had bitten him. The husband assured me that the man was mistaken and the dog was just looking for a good game of tug when he grabbed the man's pants from behind (putting it bluntly, smack on the derriere!) The husband had a set rule, handed down through the generations: Families do not keep aggressive dogs. He pointed out that the rule did not apply to his dog, however, because she had only been playing. The wife, on the other hand, felt that a bite was a bite and pointed out gently that the dog occasionally growled at her.

What could I accomplish here? The husband had his ideas about how he would respond to his dog if she bit anyone: He would hit her on the mouth to show her that she should not use her mouth on people! Then he would send her packing! Taking all of this into account, I joined by pretending that the dog had not aggressed and introduced interventions to keep the dog from "playing tug" with anyone ever again. By the second visit, when we were well on our way to resolving the problem, the husband could finally admit that the dog might have bitten the mail carrier. At that juncture, I could add long-term management strategies and more pointed interventions (that, of course, did not include hitting the dog).

As mentioned previously, it is easier to join with families whose stage of development we have experienced. If we do not understand the stage of development because we are not as far along the developmental continuum, we can try joining from what Dr. Minuchin terms a *down position*: That is, we can put the family in charge of helping us understand them and their situation.

Focus and Separation Anxiety

Assessments of families begin at the point of first contact, as do assessments of dogs. We pick up cues, starting during the initial inquiry when a family member calls to see if we are the one they want onboard to help their dog. If I get a call, for example, that a dog adopted from a shelter is showing distress over separations and has done a good bit of damage to the house, I know I had better travel quickly with a toolbox filled with hope. If the owner's property can be protected, they will be more apt to hang in there for the duration. The other critical issue is time: Will the family have enough of it?

Many dogs with separation anxiety experience even more distress when they are crated, but dogs who wreck homes lose their homes. I have had a good amount of success using a procedure that calls for crating when the owner is out of the house. I will pause here to describe the protocol for modifying separation distress and my intense focus on transitioning the dog from reliance on the owner to reliance on the crate and its contents for a sense of security while the owner is gone. Eventually, the dog should be able to handle freedom when home alone.

➢ **Relaxation and training**

> My first goal is to support the development of ultra-positive associations to known relaxers (harp music for dogs by Sue Raimond; Dog Appeasing Pheromone (DAP) products; massage by owners; Karen Overall's protocols for relaxation). All strategies should be introduced together—that is, at about the same time—and when the owners are with their dog. The environment must be soothing. The time to introduce relaxation strategies is long *before* dogs are in anxiety-producing situations.

> Nothing in Life is Free (NILIF) and similar protocols help get most dogs in a right relationship with their humans.

➢ Create a *wonderland*

Work concurrently to help dogs develop positive associations to the crate so they will relax while in it. I frame this as creating wonderlands in their crates.

The interior cushioning should be soft and comfortable. However, cushioning may have to be taken out at later stages when families start leaving the dogs home alone. If there is any possibility that the dogs will shred and ingest bedding, the bedding should be removed.

Strong reinforcers should be introduced, but only in the crate (for example, stuffed Kongs, delicious smelly treats, favorite stuffed and squeaky toys). Dogs should also be given their kibble in the crate, unless they are reluctant eaters. Relaxation strategies are employed at the same time, with the family nearby (in the same room).

If dogs with separation distress dislike crating, we go more slowly through this phase. We place kibble and treats in the back of the crate and dogs retrieve them with the door open. As soon as there is evidence of relaxation, the owners start shutting the door for a minute or two, and build up to longer stretches in which dogs are in the crate with owners present.

Success is in the details. Check to see if the dog prefers one spot over another for his crate and defer to his preferences.

➢ Increase time

We then increase the time the dogs are in their wonderlands with the door closed and the family nearby. Families leave the room for a few minutes. Eventually, owners leave the house briefly, then for longer periods. We continue using all of the relaxation strategies. Dogs should be let out of crates as soon as they appear stressed, when the family is home.

➢ "Let me in!"

Early on, dogs who have polished off all the goodies in the crate will want to get out so they can be in their preferred spots, as close as possible to their families. If the owners do not open the door and let the dogs out, the dogs will experience their crates as aversives, contraptions worth rejecting. They may dig to get out, just as they dig frantically to escape when their owners are gone.

At this point, I ask families to put renewed energy into creating wonderlands in the crate, but they reverse directions. They start by cooking a hot dog in a little light olive oil and garlic powder at a time when their dog is hungry—on the stove, not in a microwave, so the smell is irresistible. The cook puts goodies, including the hot dog or other favored food, in the crate and closes the door. The dog is on the outside trying to get in. Some dogs will work as hard to get *in* their crates as they worked to escape confinement during periods of high-anxiety. After a few minutes (while the dog is still operant, before he loses interest) the owner lets him succeed at gaining entry to wonderland in his crate. He has won at mastering the crate and its resources.

➤ **"Wonderland opens when we leave"**

The dog is now ready for the owners to create a wonderland in the crate, set the familiar stage for relaxation, but now they do not let the dog in until they are ready to walk out of the house. The owners' departure becomes the cue for the dog's favorite things to be available to him. His interest and attachment to the crate holds him while the owners are gone. Owners are instructed to leave for only a few minutes at first and build up to longer absences.

➤ **Medication**

I recommend that clients see their veterinarian about getting medication to help their dogs make the transition from anxiety to relaxation and even happiness over owner departures. Medication has its downsides, such as side effects, and it can be a challenge to find the optimal support for each dog.

There are only several dozen board certified veterinary behaviorists in the United States[3] and veterinarians have to be experts in all systems: neurology, cardiology, rheumatology, dentistry, surgery, dormatology, ophthalmology, etc., to more species than just dogs. Thus, it is difficult in some communities to find veterinarians who also know how to prescribe psychotropic medication. I handle this by providing veterinarians with leads to information about medications that have been written by known, reliable sources, such as established veterinary behaviorists. Veterinarians can also call the behavioral departments of schools of veterinary medicine for guidance. I do not recommend specific medications: I am not licensed to practice veterinary medicine. However, I do stay up-to-date on the latest research and am more than willing to do information searches for veterinarians.

➤ I encourage owners to educate themselves and report possible side effects from medication to their veterinarian. I have worked with dogs with separation anxiety who became aggressive on Clomicalm and other drugs and their veterinarians have told them that they should not stop medicating because it is unlikely that the drugs were causing the aggression. The literature often suggests otherwise.

---

[3] American College of Veterinary Behaviorists, Web: www.dacvb.org

➢ Three-way e-mail exchanges or conference calls can keep all participants working together— veterinarian, family, and consultant—until a good-enough balance is achieved for the dog. Some veterinarians will work overtime to find compatible medications for dogs.

➢ I recommend that you read the IAABCs statement on Collaborative Healthcare in the Appendix.

Families need support to work this intensively with their dogs to resolve problems that manifest themselves when no one is around to relieve dog's suffering. Veterinarians need support, too, because the first medication or a single medication as initially applied often does not create the desired effect.

➢ Over time, most veterinarians and owners will agree that medications can be withdrawn because dogs become accustomed to relaxing while their owners are away. As dogs improve, many will succeed for long periods outside the crate, alone with their Kongs, soothing music and other relaxers.

Reframing

"We may believe there is a definite truth, and

our job is to discover the truth of a situation.

But truth is a construction."

~ *Salvador Minuchin, M.D.*

Families have their own preferred explanations for why events occur. They may tell us that their dog is "really bad." Or, the dog "knows exactly what she did wrong," and "she is just jealous!" Many owners are sure their dog is "getting even" for something the owner did to them. Other families offer original explanations, for example, "Our dog is a sexist. He prefers the ladies." But, truth is a construction. Families organize their thinking about dog's problems in ways that preserve family homeostasis, or sameness, and protect their standing in society. However, if their explanations miss the target, their ensuing interventions do not work. For example, if they imagine their fear-aggressive dog is dominant and they strike the dog to force submission, the dog's aggression will likely escalate.

So often, we succeed by convincing families to change their perceptions. We introduce more scientifically based, objective views of dogs, especially if the family's constructs are interfering with problem solving.

To revisit the example above, the family who views their fear-aggressive dog as "bad" will be inclined to punish the dog, who will become more fearful and aggressive as a result. The dog behavior consultant who has worked his way into a strong leadership position might reframe by calling the dog "scared. He fears for his life. He's not bad."

At this point, you might ask, "So what is new? I always tell families what I think." However, the behavior consultant who moves in too quickly to reframe runs the risk of alienating families. A consultant might jump to a dog's defense, angrily stating, "She's not bad, she's just scared!" In doing so, she creates a dysfunctional triangle with the family, the consultant, and dog as the three legs. Instead, she must join with and win acceptance by the family as a reliable leader before the family will accept reframing. This will take a few minutes with some families and the whole session or longer with others.

In sum, families must have confidence in professionals and feel safe with them before they will yield to their explanations. Occasionally, a family never yields, no matter what. These families have boundaries that are so rigid that we can only hope for an occasional leak to get new information through.

Reframing is a powerful intervention that opens the door to new and creative solutions. Have you tried telling a family to use a soft voice and gentle movements with a dog who, in their view, is "bad" or "dominant"? We are all familiar with the problems that the "dominant dog" construct elicits for dogs. The "bad dog" image evokes anger in families and then they want to challenge their dogs. Families who tell you their dog is "dominant" will want you to teach them how to "show him who is boss" and "put him in his place." They have to come around to a view of their dog as "scared", for example, before they will be gentle and willing to use positive reinforcement. If we bring out the treats too early, they are apt to look at us with wide-eyed disbelief. We do not want to lose them. So first, we join with them, win their confidence, and earn the right to lead. It takes time for some families to acknowledge that we know what we are doing and will not get them into even deeper trouble with their dog.

A nonjudgmental approach to reframing

Animal behavior consultants embrace a nonjudgmental approach to clients and colleagues and research supports this stance. To elicit cooperation, we can reframe by characterizing situations in positive ways that focus on the dog's and the family's strengths.

As an example of how a nonjudgmental approach facilitates joining, a father cornered his dog and yelled at her. She tried to bite him. I would not have gotten far with this client if I told him he was the scary one in the situation, so I put a positive spin on their difficulties: "You are too big for her!" I observed that he had a loud voice that booms, and she might feel safe with him if he would just "tone down the boom box." I had to teach him to be nurturing and generous about reinforcing his dog, and to his credit, he did learn. If I had said the obvious—"Stop yelling at her"—the whole family would have been roused to the father's defense, at the expense of the dog.

I work with many Yorkshire Terriers, and some will greet all but their beloved person with rude, dictatorial barking that communicates, "You are not welcome here!" Other people, including family members, feel wounded because the dog does not appear to like them. I might open by musing: "Ah, another Yorkie who likes to direct traffic." My reframing enables these families to see annoying behavior in a more positive and humorous light, and from the perspective of the dog. Indeed, the guarding Yorkie might like the rest of the family just fine if she had not already picked out a special person to watch over and try so hard to keep for herself.

Reframing, in essence, means that the consultant describes what is going on in such a way that the family moves more willingly in the direction of its goals. It is seldom enough to fix problems but sometimes enough to get families unstuck and rolling again.

Enactment

As we gather information from families through questionnaires and interviews, some families present their truths in straightforward ways that intuitively make good sense to us. They somewhat understand their situation and readily allow us to enlighten them on the complexities of dogs. We show them how to fix things and go on our way. But, just as often, the truth is hidden and there are no straightforward paths from assessment to intervention. Rather, dog behavior consultants have to engage in struggles with families over whose "truth" will hold. *Whoever controls the definition of the situation controls the situation.*

During a diagnostic interview, families will describe and explain, but that does not give us all that we need to know to help them. Both consultants and families control the content of the information introduced.

Consultants may fail to ask the right questions or may ask questions that provoke defensiveness. In addition, families are typically selective about what they will conceal and reveal. They may present their dog or family in a favorable or unfavorable light, depending on the needs of the system. Therefore, consultants might want to see an enactment of what happens before drawing conclusions about what is going on.

It should be understood that we do not want to create enactments of aggressive episodes.

At various points, the consultant will ask families to demonstrate what typically occurs and families will play it out with their dogs in the consultant's presence. Home visits are invaluable because it is in the home that we get to see what actually occurs.

In addition, as mentioned previously, some families are adept at triangulating us into positions that rob us of the maneuverability we need to help them. It is usually not in their or dog's best interests to succeed at reeling us in this way. They ask for help because they are stuck, and if we go the way of the family, we will become stuck too.

Self-awareness helps us figure out when a family is drawing us in. They will signal us that we had better accommodate to them because they want us to adhere to their rules and their realities. We have to accommodate to some extent, but if we accommodate too much, we lose our advantage as leaders.

As Minuchin explains in detail in his book, *Techniques of Family Therapy*, enactment is one of the simplest interventions we can use to regain leverage.[4] That is, when we feel that we are faltering, we can suggest that family members interact with their dog to show us what they mean. This gives us opportunities to step outside the system and thus regain leadership, and with it, the control necessary to influence change.

I will give you an example of a trainer who was swept into the family reality, to the detriment of a dog. The trainer was called in to help with a young Labrador Retriever whose owners complained that he was hyperactive and destructive. The trainer discovered that the dog was spending 10 to 12 hours a day confined to a crate in the kitchen while his owners were at work. When they returned home, he was confined to the kitchen. In the evening, while the family watched television in an adjoining room, he watched them from behind a baby gate. Now, even after it was pointed out to the trainer that the dog was crated too many hours, the trainer could not see that the family's excessive use of the crate might hamper their efforts to train the dog. This family controlled the definition of the situation and blamed the dog and his breeding, and their inability to set aside enough time for training. How does the saying go? "There are none so blind as he who will not see!"

Returning to performances, I created an amusing enactment to demonstrate to a couple, on the spot, that their three seemingly incorrigible Corgis could transition from rebounding off each other to deferring to

---

[4] Minuchin, Salvador and H. Charles Fishman (1990) *Family Therapy Techniques*. Harvard University Press: Cambridge. p. 81

owner leadership, quickly. The owners would ask their dogs to pay attention, but the dogs were all over the place. I realized that this family understood positive reinforcement but did not understand that some reinforcers work a whole lot better than others. The dogs simply were not interested in their grocery store treats. To teach them quickly, because actions speak louder than words, I brought along a fresh-cooked rotisserie chicken, plunked the chicken on a table, lifted the lid, and suddenly had a captive audience. The dogs, of course, tried to figure out how to get my treasure to come to them. The family understood my message: They could get compliance quickly but they had to trump the dogs' interest in one other.

At this point, dog trainers might point out that the dogs were still not trained. Of course they were not. Regardless, the couple learned an important training principle that gave them hope: If they paid better attention to the reinforcers, they could quickly get all three dogs to focus. They did not have to spend years training each dog individually as they had feared.

Interviews: Who to Include

I know of dog behavior consultants who state from the outset that all members of a family must be present for initial consults. My rule is flexible. That is because some families are efficient and appoint one or two members to serve as problem solvers for dogs. The consultant takes the lead, the appointed member(s) takes what they learn back to the family, and the family cooperates appropriately.

However, in certain situations, it is mandatory to include whole families. It depends on how the families operate. If consensus is the rule—that is, if no one acts until everyone agrees—we must work with the whole families. If we leave a member out, or try to proceed before everyone agrees, the family, perhaps the absent member, will mobilize resistance. It is imperative that we meet with the family as a whole to discuss a dog's problems, the potential impact on family life, and solutions.

You can sometimes discern from a phone call and pre-interview behavior questionnaire that family members look to one another for agreement before making decisions. If they refer to what other family members believe they should do, and especially if it conflicts with what the caller wants the family to do, you should ask the other members to be present and possibly not proceed until they are all in the room. Members can block progress simply by being absent.

When you have the whole family present, you might want to ask each of them to tell you their views on the dog's problems and what they think should be done. You join by hearing them out.

In families where individuality is not supported—that is, everyone is expected to share opinions and differences are not welcome—families will be slow to recognize and support the separate identity and unique needs of dogs or humans. These families will more likely offer anthropomorphisms; that is, they attribute human qualities to dogs. Discrimination is the better part of valor, and the consultant must decide if challenging the family reality is going to make a difference. As noted earlier, some problems can be resolved even if families do have wrong beliefs about their dogs.

Triangulation and Cherry-Picking

One of my clients with young children had a Weimaraner puppy with a strong prey drive who was intensely interested in children's movements and had started lunging at dogs and people during his daily walks. The husband and wife solicited advice from various sources before calling me. They told me about books, videos, and recommendations from neighbors, veterinarians, trainers, and breeders. Most of it interested them, although they recognized that much of it was conflicting.

Meanwhile, the family showed some resistance to me at the outset—for example, they questioned the wisdom of using treats as reinforcers—but the husband seemed to be following my lead. I was sure of my assessment of the dog, and my behavior modification and management plans were sound. The session was going so well that I scarcely paid attention when, halfway through, the wife opted out because she did not feel well. I took her withdrawal at face value. I should have asked, is she going to support what we are doing? Because afterwards it was the wife who dismantled my plan, and then the family reverted to cherry-picking. They decided to go with treats as rewards, and the children did exercise leadership as I suggested (when the dog was chasing, they would turn quickly and ask for a sit, then reinforce it). However, they decided it made no sense to give up the choke chain or leash pops that had been sanctioned by other trainers. The family had thus far not committed to following anyone's lead. Perhaps this is what they did to feel in control? Whatever the reason, they had a penchant for cherry-picking.

Cherry-picking is a form of triangulation. I would present ideas and the family would refer to methodologies from other "experts" that were incompatible with my ideas. When they spoke with other trainers and neighbors, they similarly referred back to my thoughts.

During the second visit, I insisted that all family members be present. I did a re-run of the first session, but could not seal any deals with them. That is, they would still not commit to any unified course of action. However, this time I was ready for them; I had a plan to counteract their cherry-picking.

I was blunt. I told the parents, it is my way or the highway. They were to follow my lead exactly or I would not work with them. The problems were serious. During the time I was working with their dog, I did not want them talking to anyone about dogs or reading any dog books. Especially, I did not want them to watch charismatic trainers on television employing dubious but dazzling methods. I feared (was certain) they would be wooed. They could fire me at any time, but these were my conditions for working with them.

Notice that I said, "While I am working with your dog (not family)." I wanted distance from them and a strong boundary. Our focus had to be on the dog. I pushed away because familiarity and joining seemed to intensify their need to control and cherry-pick.

We were reasonably successful. The family never did completely stop talking about other trainers' ideas, but the dog's behavior was brought within the range of normal and tolerable. I do not know what the family did in between sessions or how much they were able to resist the temptation to solicit advice about their dog. Nevertheless, the Weimaraner survived in her home.

Relevancy and respect for the client's right to self-determination

If families are stuck and need a push, are you willing to do the pushing to get them moving again? If so, know that when families get rolling, they go their own way, not necessarily your way. Do you remember the line from the old Jim Croce song, "I Got a Name": "If you're going my way, I'll go with you"? In one form or another, families teach us the same lesson. They will move in the direction of their own natural evolution, not ours.

By natural evolution, I mean that they have values and a life thrust, and no amount of haranguing from us about "doing the right thing" will change what they are or where they wish to be. Thus, if a family has spent years "scraping the bottom of the barrel" to put their children through college, it is unlikely that they will take from their children's college money to pay expensive veterinary bills to sustain their dog. They may be willing to give time to rehabilitate a dog, but the plan that you devise for them had better not be an expensive one or you will lose their support. They will protect their dreams ahead of the family dog. Similarly, a complicated training plan will be of little use to dog owners who are providing total care for aging parents with Alzheimer's disease, or to families with preschoolers. Thus, the solutions we prescribe must be possible for families to implement.

However, families frequently say they have one intent, and then yield to others. It is also possible to awaken families to something deeper. For example, a middle-aged couple told me they wanted to return their newly adopted fear-aggressive dog to the shelter. They felt duped because they had specifically told the shelter that they could not handle aggression and workers assured them that the dog did not have issues. Her growling and snapping was too much for them; they were ready to end the relationship. I felt the only path through the problem was for me to accept, respect, and support their decision. I also showed them how fear-aggressive dogs can be rehabilitated. For a few days, they were intent on returning the dog, but in the end, these deeply caring people could not bring themselves to turn her over to an uncertain fate. Something within them stirred, they took action, and in the end, we did successfully rehabilitate the dog. If I had tried to talk them out of their initial decision to return her, they would not have worked through their anger and disappointment and then redirected their energies to meet the dog's needs.

One issue for the dog was that she had been spayed just before being rehomed, and this appears to have negatively affected her adjustment. She went on to become the dog of their dreams. Nevertheless, I question the wisdom of spaying and neutering while dogs are in transition to new homes.

Intensity

As we have seen, simple communication may not be enough to inspire some families to act. If we talk and families do not hear us, we can try varying the intensity of our messages. We might talk very quietly and seriously, so they have to strain to listen to our apparently urgent messages. Alternatively, we can create drama using big movements. And, we can present messages forcefully to communicate that the problems are very serious and they must act.

If families do not like what we say, they will put red flags up to tell us to stop. When families signal us, it is usually wise to heed their warnings and back off. Occasionally, however, we might want to encourage a continuation of transactions even after the rules of families indicate that they have heard enough. Let us say that a family is signaling us that they are not interested in medication for their dogs with separation anxiety. We might push a little harder because we are confident that medication is needed to turn problems around, and we sense that they might rise to the challenge if we persist. Families are stressed when we ask them to maintain a transaction longer than is their habit, but going beyond comfortable bounds may be enough to inspire them to act.

Our goal with any of these interventions is to ensure that families gain new information, despite family preferences for relying on old information. Again, our push must be in directions families are willing to go.

An extreme but real-life example is a 120-pound Akita mix who bit a family member severely while in an altercation with another dog, resulting in her hospitalization. Afterwards, the owners allowed a teenager to be in a kennel run with him and the dog he fights with; I am certain that the young man could have been killed that day. Meanwhile, back in the home, the dog crowded the couple's bed and the couple would not think of asking him to move. In fact, the thought of telling the dog to do anything brought the wife to tears; she loved him so much that she did not want to interfere with his natural movement. The dog occasionally ran out the door of the house and to the neighbors. Thus far, the neighbors had not been outside when this occurred. Throughout the interview, I sat very still because I was afraid of what the dog would do to me if I moved. He barked at my side and went up my arm to within inches of my face. (I did not know the dog had issues with people until I met him, or I would have asked the owners to have him on a leash and at a distance from me.) In spite of all of this, the owners told me they loved him and could not imagine a life without him, they would be so sad.

In his lifetime, the Akita mix had little socialization. He was not asked to do anything but eat and choose his preferred sleeping spots. The owners organized their lives around his wants. I envisioned him killing someone, so I used intensity to turn the "thermostat" way up, so the family would make the connection. We turn up the thermostat when we tell families what is likely to happen if their dog bites again, when we instruct them on dog bite laws, when we ask for their permission to write letters to their veterinarians so others are aware of our concerns about their dogs, and when we describe worst-case scenarios. This is the scariest experience I have ever had with a family. I did recommend euthanasia and referred the dog to a veterinary behaviorist, who also recommended euthanasia.

A less dramatic example is the family who thinks some puppy behaviors are adorable, but we know that the charm will not hold through adolescence. We want them to envision what the behavior will look like in a few months and to understand that it is easier to modify behaviors now than to wait until they are no longer cute. Conversely, if a family is thinking about sending their dog back to a shelter, we might help them imagine a bright day ahead when the dog's problems are resolved. These interventions put pressure on families to move in the direction of their stated goals.

I brought intensity to bear on the family who was cherry-picking with the Weimaraner as a form of triangulation. "It is my way or the highway" is a powerful gauntlet to throw down on a family. I use this strategy only when I can think of no gentler way to meet my ethical obligations to dogs and families.

Boundary-Making and Unbalancing

Sometimes we must "upset apple carts" or risk not being of help. Suppose a wife is appropriately concerned for a dog, but the husband grumbles and maintains his distance. You may conclude that the wife is the "nicer person." However, if you look closer, you may find a semi-functional triangle. That is, the wife's role is that of a rescuer and she unconsciously pushes other members away when they try to help with the dog. If you try to get the husband involved, she blocks the husband and you from effecting any change. In fact, spouses often form coalitions with dogs that keep the other spouse shut out of the dyadic relationship (spouse and dog dyad).

In this situation, the husband is, on some level, relieved because the dog is meeting his wife's needs and he does not have to work as hard at the marriage. He may not be comfortable with intimacy and the "problem dog" gets him off the hook.

I worked with a Yorkshire Terrier who guarded his most precious possession, the wife, from her husband. This was tolerated for years, in mild form. However, when the Yorkie advanced to biting the husband for approaching his wife, the wife also grew dissatisfied with her relationship with the dog. My goal in this case was to reel the husband in and help the husband and wife form a stronger coalition that did not exclude the dog, but that regulated the dog's access to the wife. For example, the wife started tethering the dog just before the husband arrived home from work. The dog was allowed on the bed, but if he growled the wife put him in a crate for a little while (a few minutes is usually enough). The husband fed the dog especially high-value treats (chicken, cheese, egg whites). Soon, the threesome could coexist again, with the husband and wife a stronger unit because they were not allowing the dog to intrude as much.

With some couples, one spouse will over-function while the other under-functions. That is, a wife may be totally committed to housetraining the puppy, takes her to training classes, teaches the children to interact with her appropriately, gets up at night; whereas the husband, when left alone with the dog, fails to put her out at regular intervals and does not reinforce any training. He then complains that the dog is not trained.

You will not be successful if you try to get the husband to do more. Rather, you will affect recovery from this dysfunctional pattern if you convince the over-functioner to tone down, or stop working so hard, until the poorly functioning spouse steps up to the plate. With support from you, the over-functioning wife described above can let the husband know what she wants from him. She can tell him, for example, that the dog is staying, no matter what. If he does not comply, she does just enough so the dog does not suffer. In most cases, after problems have escalated to crisis proportions, the husband will be stirred to action!

Our goal might be to get the spouses working together, flexibly, to solve their problems. It will be tempting to characterize one spouse as "good" and the other as "lazy" and the source of the problem, but remember that over-functioning/underfunctioning and, similarly, over-adequate/inadequate, are reciprocal patterns with not one, but both parties responsible. It is possible that the inactive spouse has tried to help before, but was rebuffed by a take-charge spouse. Whatever the reason, *it is far easier to inspire an over-functioning spouse to tone down than to convince an under-functioning spouse to put forth more energy.* The good news is that even a slight decrease in over-functioning and a slight increase from the under-functioner can make a difference and restore flexibility, so the family can work together to resolve problems[5]. It should be emphasized again that the over-function/under-function pattern is a reciprocating mechanism, and both parties participate to keep it in place.

Remember, too, that families can benefit from the role demands of having a dog who requires a lot of attention because of behavioral issues. We may find a

---

[5] Kerr, Michael, (1981) "Family Systems Theory and Therapy." Chapter 7, *Handbook of Family Therapy.* Edited by Alan S. Gurman, and David P. Kniskern, Brunner/Mazel: New York. p. 244-245

husband or wife who brings much energy to problem solving—but does not follow through to the point that the problem is actually resolved. In families that "sputter out," you might find that the dog's problems stabilize structures and the family will become dys-functional again when the dog improves and the role demands change.

A central notion is *fit,* and along with that, *how does the family benefit from having a dog with problems?*

Conversely, have you ever struggled along with a family when suddenly they see the light and the problems are quickly resolved because the family has a new challenge? There are sluggish families who will suddenly become competent with their dogs (and children) when, say, an aging parent becomes ill and requires constant care. They no longer needed a dog (or child) with problems to maintain homeostasis; they have the aging parent to stabilize the system. ■

Chapter 6

Person
of the Animal Behavior
Consultant

The Truth about Positive
Regard and Respect
for Differences

1. We prefer spending time with colleagues and
    clients who view the world as we do. Ralph
    Waldo Emerson wrote, "'Do you love me?' actu-
    ally means 'Do you see the same truth?'" C.S.
    Lewis added, ". . . Or at least, do you care about
    the same truth?" It is food for the soul when
    people care about the same truth as we do.

2. As animal care professionals, we are being paid to facilitate problem solving, not to find soul mates. Clients do not have to be of the same mind as us for us to help them.

3. When is it that we are able to work most effectively with clients? You might say, "It is when we understand the problem at hand. If an animal has separation anxiety, for example, then we are at our best when we understand separation distress." Yes, that is true, but we can learn about separation anxiety by educating ourselves about it through reading. This is not the same as having the self-awareness and emotional maturity that we need to assess reliably and connect assessments with appropriate interventions.

4. It takes much thought and energy, over time, to arrive at a clear understanding of where we stand on issues. We are at our best with clients when we are able to be clear about where we stand on issues of importance to dogs and dog-family relationships.

5. A strong leader knows how to state their case with clients and colleagues: "This is who I am, this is what I believe, this is where I stand, and this is the line I will not cross." The well-defined leader does not see himself as "keeper of the truth." However, he knows *his* truth. He respects the right of others to arrive at their own conclusions. He says, "This is what I believe," but he does not implicitly or explicitly say, "This is what you must believe or I will not respect you."

6. To lead successfully, we must join with people, enter into their world, speak from their perspective, respect their values, understand them, and be sensitive to both dog and human's needs. Families will discern if we care about them as well.

7. One value we should bring to our work is positive regard or respect for others. Positive regard helps us to connect with clients and colleagues, despite differences.

Personal Growth

"Know thyself."

~ Socrates

"The unexamined life is not worth living."

~ Plato

In this section, I introduce concepts and skills that will help you work more effectively with families. Most of the ideals espoused here are aspirational—that is, our lives are improved and we enhance the lives of those around us as we develop personal qualities that research shows improves outcomes in helping relationships.

In the first section, I will discuss emotional maturity and the various dimensions associated with the *use of self.*

Emotional maturity

Most of the animal behavior consultants that I know aspire to respond to life's challenges in high-minded ways. Mature action is good for our self-esteem and a gift to those who live in relationships with us, animals included. Immaturities are understandable but a drain on resources. This is because of the correlations between maturity and efficient problem solving. I will posit that professionals and families who have evolved are more functional: They can get things done; they reach to meet the next challenge; they can change with change.

Adults who do not outgrow childish behaviors are said to be immature. They might be selfishly preoccupied with their own needs and not as interested in the needs of others. If we thwart them, they will see themselves as victims of our behavior in spite of evidence to the contrary. If we do not go their way, they may harbor resentments or vindictively seek revenge. If these behaviors are part of an overall pattern, they may point to a personality disorder such as narcissism or borderline.

What does immaturity look like in families and other social systems? Members rigidly adhere to old behavior patterns with minimal yield. They do not take the time to consider the probable consequences of their actions in light of what they want to achieve, so when they do react, they do so impulsively.

Now, let us be honest. Most of us probably recognize ourselves in these descriptions, if only a little. We are deeply into our lives; having families and a profession necessitates that we evolve to meet complex challenges. As such, we surely have moments of immaturity because growth is not achieved without regression. This means that, on the path to self-definition (who are we?), we might return to earlier behaviors to resoundingly reject them as we add new and more functional behaviors to our repertoire.

Differentiation of self

Bowen contributed the concept *differentiation of self* to help us understand emotional maturity and self-definition from a family systems theory perspective.

"The differentiation of self concept describes the fact that people are not the same in terms of the way they manage individuality and togetherness in their lives. People can be viewed as existing on a continuum, a continuum called the *scale of differentiation*, ranging from the lowest to the highest levels of differentiation of self."[1] People with higher levels of differentiation of self know what they believe and why. They are able to state their case: "This is who I am and what I believe, and this is the point beyond which I will not go." To the degree to which solid self exists within the individual, it permits him not to be totally at the mercy of emotional pressures from the group to think and act in certain ways. It is that part of the individual's functioning that is not dependent on relationships systems to support it.[2]

Bowen used the term "solid self" to describe the portion of self where the beliefs are strong and remain non-negotiable under pressure from the family and other relationship systems.

Bowen also observed that people can come across as better defined than they really are. He called this artificial front "pseudoself." Pseudoself can look a lot like solid self. An individual might say, "This is who I am and what I believe," but there are "discrepancies between what the person says and what he or she actually does when under pressure from the relation-

---

[1,2] Kerr, Michael, M.D., (1981) "Family Systems Theory and Therapy", in *Handbook of Family Therapy,* edited by A. Gurman and D. Kniskern. Brunner/Mazel: New York. p. 247

ship system. Pseudoself *is* negotiable. It is easily given up under pressure."[3]

It is also pseudoself when individuals present themselves as principled but invariably take positions *contrary* to the group. Their need to occupy adversarial positions overrides their objectivity. An example of pseudoself can be seen with some animal rights activists who are dogmatically attached to their positions and are inflammatory in their presentations. They disqualify themselves when they present conjecture as fact.

Solid self is arrived at through more intellectual, objective processes. Individuals with solid self understand that reality is a perspective. They are realistic about the relative strengths and weaknesses of their positions. These people recognize that competing points of view have legitimacy, too. Partially on this basis, they are able to maintain respect for those with whom they have philosophical differences.

Individuals at the higher end of the differentiation-of-self measure are more comfortable with diversity. In fact, the ability to tolerate difference and gain from it is at the heart of a high level of differentiation of self.[4]

[3] Kerr, Michael, M.D., (1981) "Family Systems Theory and Therapy", in *Handbook of Family Therapy,* edited by A. Gurman and D. Kniskern. Brunner/Mazel: New York. p. 247

[4] Kerr, Michael, M.D., (1981) "Family Systems Theory and Therapy", in *Handbook of Family Therapy,* edited by A. Gurman and D. Kniskern. Brunner/Mazel: New York. p. 246-247

Bowen maintains that each of us carries around opinions and beliefs that we borrowed from family, friends, books, newspapers, experts, and pseudo experts. If you want to grow in self-awareness and differentiation of self, you should ask yourself, how committed are you to these ideas? Would you yield some beliefs if you had concrete evidence that they were not valid, even if you have held the beliefs for most of your life and your whole family adheres to them?

Bowen postulates that families at the lower end of the differentiation-of-self scale are prone to get into more difficulty because, "to use a football metaphor, they lack individuals capable of making the big play. They lack the calm leader or leaders who can step forward at critical times and define a direction based on principle. Instead, these families are constantly *awash in a sea of emotionality.*"[5]

Also according to Dr. Murray Bowen, the ideas to which we have the strongest emotional attachment are the ones we are the most reluctant to give up. This is true for client families as well.

Family systems theory concepts help us understand why clients and colleagues seem to follow our lead most readily when we convey calmly that we know what we believe and why.

---

[5] Kerr, Michael, M.D., (1981) "Family Systems Theory and Therapy", in *Handbook of Family Therapy,* edited by A. Gurman and D. Kniskern. Brunner/Mazel: New York. p. 246-247

Use of self:
Empathy and self-awareness

Perhaps the most important insight that I can give you about empathy is that it is not the same as sympathy. The sympathetic person feels sorry for people. He recognizes that they are at a disadvantage and feels compassion and pity for their misfortune and distress. A little sympathy is okay but few of us would enjoy being the object of sympathy for long.

Empathy, on the other hand, does not look down but reaches across and takes us in. Empathetic persons identify with us and understand our situation, feelings and motives. They share our experiences, feel our pain, and because of them we are less alone in the world.

Is it possible to succeed in a behavior consulting practice without empathy? Perhaps it is. I know of practitioners who are skillful with dogs but cannot seem to bridge in a meaningful way with humans. Nevertheless, consultants who are able to connect empathically and convey to clients that they are both with and for them, surely make better companions for the journey.

Examples of low-empathy and high-empathy responses to clients

➢ **Deft diversions**

> *Client:* . . . and then Puddle peed on my mother's brand new carpet, right in front of her!
>
> *Consultant:* Oh. How is Puddle's appetite?

➢ **The superiority game**

> *Client*: He growls at my son, runs, and hides when I tell him to come to me.
>
> *Consultant*: The problem is, you have spoiled him.
>
> *Client:* Well, we might spoil him a little.
>
> *Consultant:* Show him who is boss and he'll be fine!

➢ **A judgmental response**

> *Client*: Max snapped at the repairman.
>
> *Consultant:* Well, why didn't you keep him tied up when you had visitors? He could have bitten someone!

> ## Irrelevancies

> *Client:* I am afraid to take Fluffy to classes for training. She is so tiny that another dog might bite her.

> *Consultant*: Oh, there are some wonderful classes just up the street. Ask for Eileen, she is a great instructor. I would call right away, though. Eileen is popular and her classes book early. . . .

> ## False reassurance

> *Client*: I am worried because Al, our Labrador Retriever, tears up the house and eats bushes. I can't leave him unsupervised for five minutes. We call him Doctor De-Structo. Frankly, my husband wants him out of the house.

> *Consultant:* Oh, he will be fine. Young Labs are over-exuberant. He will outgrow it.

> ## The psychoanalyst

> *Client:* We have a Great Dane and he's food-obsessed! He is always looking for another meal.

> *Consultant:* He probably did not get enough food as a puppy. Does anyone in your family have an eating disorder?

Examples of good-enough empathic responses:

Client: We got Frankie from rescue a week ago and spent all our spare time with him. Last night he was chewing on a rawhide and he growled at me. I am quite upset. I told rescue we could not handle a dog with aggression. We have been so good to him. We cannot believe he treated us like this.

Consultant: Ouch! It especially hurts knowing that you have been there for him. What a disappointment it must be that Rescue didn't catch on during temperament testing that he has issues! I am sure it's upsetting.

Client: Yes, we even wrote on our application that we absolutely did not want an aggressive dog! Moreover, we spent $600 on his medical care. Though he is so sweet most of the time. We really love him. Oh, but we cannot have a dog who bites!

Consultant: It is hard, I know. You have every right to take him back, and I will support you if you return him. But I can probably help you with this. I know you did not agree to take on a project. I respect your choice either way.

Client: (Couple looks at each other) We can't handle this. It is too much for us. My mother is ill . . .

Consultant: I understand.

(A week later . . . the client calls the consultant).

Client: We decided to keep him. We love him. Will you help us?

Consultant: Yes! There is something wonderful about him, isn't there? I will try to get out there right away.

If you wish to become more empathic, work on developing self-awareness. Pay attention to the centuries-old maxim from Socrates, "Know thyself."

Empathy and self-awareness are intertwined. We have to know where we begin and end and what feelings, thoughts, beliefs, and values belong to us and what belongs to the people and animals we serve.

In my opinion, *self-awareness is the second most powerful tool we can carry.* (I will describe the first shortly.) Think about it: If you are doing a consult and feel afraid, how will you know if the dog or family typically interacts in ways that elicit helpless fear in people? Alternatively, there might be something in your life experience that causes you to be afraid in situations that warrant trust. On the other hand, what if you have been interacting with a family for a while and start losing your confidence? Is it possible that the family also interacts with the dog in ways that subtly undermines the dog's confidence? Alternatively, could it be that it is typical of you to lose confidence midstream? When you are with a hardworking family do you tend to work harder too, or do you show them what needs to be done and recede? Your relationship decisions have a powerful impact on the outcome of cases.

Are you an attentive listener? Do you have a strong ethical foundation? Do you know what you value? If you do not know your values, how will you discern when your client's values are not the same as yours?

Positive regard

The most important tool in our toolbox is positive regard or respect for clients (animal and human), colleagues (including those with whom we disagree), and self. It is beyond the scope of this book to show all the research that supports positive regard as an essential value in helping relationships, but I will amplify by referring to one study that yielded interesting results. Reportedly, there were "strong indications that the communication of human warmth and understanding are the principle vehicles for communicating respect."[6] Thus, we show respect when we try to understand. We might ask, "Do I hear you saying . . .?" or "Do you mind explaining . . . ?" Conversely, we are disrespectful when we cut speakers off prematurely or pick out a small portion of their message and go to war against it.

---

[6] Pierce, R. Counselor respect. (1967) In R. R. Carkhuff (Ed.), *The counselor's contributions to facilitative processes.* Parkinson: Urbana, Ill.

Values
and Value Differences

"A value is an organized system of attitudes.

Values provide us with guidelines for

behavior . . . they direct our behavior so that it

is consistent with the achievement of goals we

have."

~ *Joseph DeVito*

Rokeach, who wrote the book *The Nature of Human Values*, identified two kinds of values: terminal and instrumental. *Terminal* values have to do with goals and principles that guide us towards achieving our goals. *Instrumental* values reflect our vision for how we will reach our goals.

To enhance self-awareness and other-awareness, I recommend that you take the Rokeach Value Survey and compare your values with the values of individuals in other professions, religions, societies. The Rokeach book (see bibliography) is available in most public libraries; also, the test and some results can be found on the Internet.

Examples of terminal values are:
> A comfortable life
> A sense of accomplishment
> Pleasure

Mature love
Self-respect
Wisdom
Social recognition

Examples of instrumental values are:
Ambitious
Broadminded
Capable
Cheerful
Intellectual
Imaginative
Responsible

How We Err

Practitioners who are new to the field typically approach consults with trepidation: "What if I make a mistake?" Experienced consultants know they will err in ways that thwart progress, but they are confident that they and their clients will recover.

Clients do not always let us know when we have erred, so it can be a challenge to figure out what has to be fixed.[7] With that in mind, in this section I will identify common pitfalls and hope this helps the reader avoid some of them.

---

[7] Odell, M., T.J. Butler, and M.B. Dielman (1997) *Client experiences of solution focused couple therapy.* Paper presented at the 55th Annual American Association for Marriage and Family Therapy Conference

➢ *The timing is off*

We will falter if we press for change prematurely. This happens when we feel that we have joined sufficiently and are confident that we are in the lead. We think that we have a handle on the problem and see what needs to be done to achieve results. However, the family is not ready for us. We misread their signals. Perhaps the family seemed impressed with our insights and eager to start . . . except for one member and that individual is the one who happens to control movement in the family. When this occurs, we have to backtrack to win support from the recalcitrant member.

In another scenario, the timing might be off because the consultant moves in with solutions before letting the family vent about their troubles with their dog.

The most common mistake probably occurs when a family uses a tool or method that we would not and we tell them so before they are joined with us sufficiently to withstand the strain of differing opinions. The family is polite but concludes that we are not the expert they want in their home. They marginalize us in their minds (and in the minds of their neighbors, to whom they complain when we are not around. A study by the Technical Assistance Research Program demonstrated that satisfied consumers tell four to five other customers about their experiences. Dissatisfied customers tell an average of nine to ten people.)[8]

➢ *Too much or too little*

A family might have a big problem and our plan is too small. Suppose the dog is suffering from separation distress and we recommend a Dog Appeasing Pheromone (DAP) Diffuser and a stuffed Kong. These can be useful if combined with many (no less than a dozen) other appropriate interventions, but fall flat on their own.

On the other hand, we can do too much. If a dog eliminates in the house and jumps up on visitors, the family should not have to invest in months of obedience training to get satisfactory results with their dog.

The common result of bad timing and bad-fit interventions is usually that clients are reasonably positive about us but there is not much movement and nobody is sure why.

➢ *My way is right*

Mistakes occur when we embrace a training model or belief system too ardently and try to fit dogs and families to our model instead of searching for the model that fits the families who are at the table with us. We might be fluid in the model's language and capable of presenting our case eloquently, but

---

[8] Cost of dissatisfaction. A study by the Technical Assistance Research Program (TARP) in Washington, D.C.,

to fit it to every family we will have to overlook key elements of the case.

We can recover from mistakes of this type if they are caught early enough. If they are not, the consulting relationship simply ends because clients will cancel out.

As an example, a Skinnerian behaviorist might deny that dogs have emotions that drive their behavior. Some might acknowledge that dogs do emote, but they maintain that dog's feelings are irrelevant and talking about feelings impedes progress. What happens if a family persists in describing their dog's problems, not in terms of observed behavior, but in terms of the dog's fears, grief, and anxieties (emotions)? If the behaviorist says, "dogs do not grieve" or "how your dog feels does not matter," the family will not have confidence in their ability to understand them or their dog.

It is usually not very hard to catch consultants who are showing this type of bias. They discuss their theoretical preferences overtly and are good at crossing off options that do not fit with their ideology. They are not as successful as their models would suggest they should be with cases that do not fit with their ideologies.

➢ *Philosophical differences*

The type of mistake that is of greatest concern is the *philosophical*. This is where a fundamental discrepancy occurs between the consultant and the clients over basic values and orientations to living with a companion animal. Figuring out that there is such a problem may sound easy, but it is not easy in practice because the underlying values that orient people's lives are usually not explicitly articulated. In addition, we tend to assume a greater degree of commonality than may actually exist between client families and ourselves, especially if the clients seem similar to us in some ways.

The consultant who is prone to philosophical mistakes has rather strong reactions to clients and colleagues who do not share their assumptions. They are reluctant to change their underlying agenda to achieve an outcome, even in the face of client wishes. These consultants are apt to believe that they know what is in families and dogs best interests, and are committed to seeing that outcome through. The arguments made in service of the consultant's agenda may be quite sound—their pre-existing assumptions might have validity. However, such a choice may be ill advised or ill suited for some families; the families know this and, having minds of their own, plot their escape from professionals with agendas. Unfortunately, families might at this point give up on their search for compatible, qualified help for their dogs.

Social Change and Triangulation

Most of us want our lives to count for something. According to the enormously effective social activist Martin Luther King, "If a man hasn't discovered something that he will die for, he isn't fit to live."[9] He also stated that, "The ultimate measure of a man is not where he stands in moments of comfort and convenience, but where he stands at moments of challenge and controversy."[10] That said, social movements fall prey to dysfunctional triangulation that ends up serving the "opposition" better than the cause. I will outline here three types of activity that are typically employed and mitigate against change:

> ➤ **Negative campaigning**

As agents on the high road to social change, we would do well to keep our focus on issues, not individuals. Successful activists, and truly successful leaders (humanitarians), bridge with others in spite of differences; they do not have a need to be against anyone. They are passionate about creating opportunities for their own but do not work against opportunity for others. In sum, they have the others in mind, even those with whom they have differences. Their goal is to promote their ideas, not to do away with resisters.

---

[9] Martin Luther King, Jr., speech, Detroit, Michigan, June 23, 1963.
[10] Martin Luther King, Jr., *Strength to Love, 1963*

It is easy to spot negative campaigners. They do not stop at being against the "opposition" but turn against their own over differences that the more open-minded among us would consider insignificant. Positive campaigners are able to appreciate others as unique entities with the same rights they have: To add things up in their own way, to define where they stand on the issues as only they can, and to emerge as unique beings who aspire to contribute by being most fully themselves and no one else.

Negative campaigning is, of course, a form of triangulation and negative campaigners feed the opposition. This is partially because others, irrespective of their stance on the issues, are offended by their tactics. One might argue that those who protest most vehemently will be least effective at influencing social change, though they make the most noise.

➤ Coercion

Face it; most of us do not like to be told what to do. We want to look at the evidence and draw our own conclusions and determine for ourselves the appropriate actions. We are not apt to respond well if others try to force their conclusions on us. In sum, we resist coercive approaches that put us in fear of negative consequences if we do not fall in line. The consequences might be:

> "If you do not agree with us, we will not respect you."

> "If you do not do as we would do, we will tell others and they will shun you."

If you are interested in effecting social change, I suggest that you commit to respecting deeply those who you wish to influence. Disrespect and shunning are forms of triangulation and leave in their wake layers of dysfunction. Negative campaigning and coercion send potential supporters scurrying to the "other side".

> **Exaggeration**

Are you prone to exaggerate? Let us say you are against a method like alpha rolls and you want your colleagues and client families to be against them as well. In fact, you want them eradicated, wiped off the face of the training landscape. My advice to you is to let go of the emotional drama. Colleagues and clients will not trust you if you draw them into an emotion-laden triangle between them (the naïve or ill informed), alpha role proponents and holdouts (the bad guys), and people like yourself (true advocates for dogs). Most of us do not have a need to view animal professionals using outdated practices as incompetent or uncaring. If you insist on describing yesterday's practices in terrible terms, I ask you, what are your goals? Just tell us we do not need the alpha roll in our toolbox anymore. Tell us why. Show us the research and theory that supports your conclusion . . . without the emotionality about the injustice that has been done to all the dogs who have been subject to alpha rolls and other practices that used to make sense, even to you.

I will argue here that extremism and militancy are forms of exaggeration and extremists thwart progress because others, to protect their integrity and autonomy, will be stirred to resist their influence. As such, they make it more difficult for moderates to usher in middle-ground changes. ∎

Appendix A

Study Questions

Note: Readers may contact the Standards Commission of the International Association of Animal Behavior Consultants (IAABC) about handing study question answers in for review[1]

1. List three examples of traits in humans that seem to remain stable over time and are not determined solely by the environment.

2. List three examples of traits in dogs that remain reasonably stable over time and, while they might be environmentally influenced, are not determined solely by the environment.

3. List six examples of rules families might have that affect dogs.

4. List three examples of roles dogs are allowed to fill in some families but not in others.

5. What do we mean when we say that in some families, consensus is the rule?

---

[1] International Association of Animal Behavior Consultants (IAABC), www.iaabc.org . E-mail: Standards@iaabc.org

6. What are emotional triangles?

7. What is triangulation?

8. What is the value of a flexible triangle?

9. When is triangulation dysfunctional?

10. Describe two types of triangles that occur.

11. Describe two situations where the dog is the third leg of a triangle.

12. What is a stable coalition?

13. What is a healthy alternative to triangulation?

14. According to Dr. Murray Bowen, what is the role of anxiety in triangulation

15. What function does rejection serve in triangulation?

16. Who is responsible for the emotional triangles and the dysfunction that ensues?

17. Briefly, when is a family functional?

18. As a dog behavior consultant, what is your responsibility to families? What is your responsibility to dogs?

19. Explain how some of a dog's behavior problems might be caused by families?

20. Explain why a family might not have primary responsibility for a dog's problems?

21. Name a phase of the family lifecycle. What has to be accomplished developmentally during that phase?

22. What might cause a family to balk at moving along the developmental continuum?

23. What might happen to the family that is stuck?

24. What might happen to individuals who are stuck and, as a result, do not move along developmentally?

25. What might happen to dogs who are not able to move along the developmental continuum with their families?

26. What phase of the family lifecycle are you in? What are you doing to navigate it successfully?

27. At what phase of the family lifecycle are dogs most likely to be surrendered to shelters? Why is that?

28. In what phase of family life are owners most concerned with how they are doing at puppy rearing? Why?

29. List six ways in which dogs can enhance family life.

30. How might dogs detract from family life?

31. What phase(s) have you not yet experienced? What can you do that will help you assess fami-

lies whose life experience you do not understand?

32. What is "joining" and how does it affect the
    helping process?

33. When might you tell a client family stories
    about your own dogs?

34. What is "reframing"?

35. When might you use reframing to facilitate
    change?

36. What is an "enactment"?

37. When might you ask for an enactment?

38. What is one strategy you might use to work
    successfully with families where consensus is
    the rule?

39. Why respect the client's right to self-
    determination?

40. What is "intensity" and how might you vary
    intensity to effect change?

41. What is unbalancing? Give an example that
    shows why you might want to unbalance a sys-
    tem to encourage problem solving.

42. What is empathy? What is the difference be-
    tween empathy and sympathy?

43. How are self-awareness and empathy related?

44. What do your clients value? What do you value?

45. What are some of your *solid-self* beliefs? Your *pseudoself* beliefs?

46. Have you made up your mind about every dog and dog-owner relationship issue? What are the key issues and what activities will you engage in to help you further define your beliefs?

47. What social norms, if any, would you like to change? What strategies might you use to influence change?

Appendix B

Collaborative
Healthcare Model

International Association of
Animal Behavior Consultants

The IAABC supports a Collaborative Healthcare Model that promotes seamless cooperation and an exchange of usable information between the animal behavior consultant, client, veterinarian, applied animal behaviorist, trainer, and/or veterinary behaviorist. Groomers, breeders, extended family, etc., may also be included in the loop, depending on the issues.

This is different from the model of old that says, "Refer to a veterinarian first to rule out medical issues before starting any consult". Rather, animal behavior consultants optimize opportunities to help animals by establishing relationships with client families and by facilitating referrals. Animal behavior consultants do what they can to ensure that clients travel informed and veterinarians have the information they need to make decisions. This may mean that the animal behavior consultant sends the client to a veterinarian or veterinary behaviorist with a written report, establishes contact by phone, or provides usable information in the form of articles with state-of-the-art information in them. The client gets where they need to go, but with support from the animal behavior consultant, and the animal behavior consultant provides colleagues with usable information.

Animal Behavior Consultants do not advise on medical issues, drugs or diet. However, they may research and make information from known reliable sources available to clients, colleagues and veterinarians. Reliable sources include leading members of the veterinary and veterinary behavior community and peer-reviewed journals and similarly trusted publications.

June, 2006
Check for updates on web:
www.iaabc.org/collaborative_care.htm

Appendix C

Web Resources

reliable sources of information on dogs and links to dog products

American Association for Marriage and Family Therapy
Web: www.aamft.org
Articles, Therapist Locator.net

Clicker Solutions
Web: www.clickersolutions.com
Articles

Dog Bite Law
Web: www.dogbitelaw.com
Articles and solid information

Douglas Island Veterinary Service
Web: home.gci.net/~divs/index.htm
Articles on behavior, training, nutrition, diseases

Harp Music by Sue Raimond
Web: www.petpause2000.com
PET PAUSE is a harp music designed to provide en-richment/complementary therapy for pets and people

Ian Dunbar
Web: www.jamesandkenneth.com
Articles: new puppy, new adult dog, behavior problems

International Association of Animal Behavior Consultants
Web: www.iaabc.org
State of the art articles and standards, and regional Consultant Locator

International Veterinary Information Service
Web: www.ivis.org
Original, up-to-date publications, proceedings of veterinary meetings, continuing education

Kong Company
http://www.kongcompany.com
Articles on the creative use of Kongs

Latka's Training Treats
Web: www.de-licioustreats.com
Wholesome, all natural, award winning treats

Lynn Hoover
Web: DogQuirks.com
Articles, book orders

Mar Vista Animal Medical Center
Web: www.marvistavet.com/index.html
Articles on training, behavior, healthcare

Premier
Web: www.premier.com
Easy Walk harness, Gentle Leader Headcollar, Ultimate Puppy Toolkit

References on Separation Anxiety–
UC Davis, University of California
www.vetmed.ucdavis.edu/CCAB/separation.html
Links to reliable information on separation anxiety in dogs

Steve Dale Pet World
Web: www.stevedalepetworld.com
Articles on today's issues by activist and media great Steve Dale. He serves as a bridge to pet owners, advancing state of the art methods and modern technologies

St. Hubert's Animal Welfare Center
Web: www.sthuberts.org
Behavior and training articles

Paws-Up
Web: http://www.paws-up.net
Assistance and therapy dog training, education and support. Home to award-winning newsletter

Web Designer Sheri Huffman
Web: http://www.virtualhelpinghand.com
Gifted designer of the IAABC web site, www.iaabc.org and dogquirks.com. Cover design for book

GLOSSARY

for words not defined in the text

Activist. Works for social change. An activist can be a militant reformer, or a dedicated advocate for social transformation, with extreme or moderate views.

Alpha roll. Pinning a dog on its back. In theory, this is supposed to communicate to dogs that humans doing the rolls are Alpha in charge, not the dogs. The theory has largely been discredited but dogs are still getting Alpha rolled.

Anxiety. A state of uneasiness, apprehension, and fear.

Arousal. A general state of alertness that follows from sensory stimulation.

Aversives. Refers to unpleasant, painful or otherwise punishing stimuli, as perceived by the organism; it typically results in avoidance of the stimuli.

Bipolar disorder. A mood disorder, with highs (hypomanic or manic episodes) characterized by periods of inflated self-esteem or grandiosity, decreased need for sleep, pressure to keep talking (many e-mails, phone calls), distractibility. Highs are inter-spersed with periods of depression or moods may be mixed.

Borderline personality disorder. A pattern of unstable and intense interpersonal relationships characterized by alternations between the extremes of idealization and devaluation; borderlines engage in frantic efforts to avoid abandonment. The disorder is also characterized by impulsivity, unstable self-images, emotional reactivity, and chronic feelings of emptiness. In addition, inappropriate, intense anger or difficulty controlling anger.[1]

Boundaries. As defined by Minuchin, "The bounda-ries of a system are the rules defining who participates and how." Boundaries serve like fences to control interaction within and between systems.

Cherry-picking. Metaphorically, refers to the ten-dency of some families to choose from among the best and pass on some less attractive options that are as essential to the success of a behavior consultant's behavior modification and training plans.

Construct. A concept or schematic idea.

Context. The circumstances in which an event occurs.

Contextual. A term used to refer to the social envi-ronment that is both a part of and the setting for an event.

---

[1] Diagnostic Criteria from DMS-IV. American Psychiatric Associa-tion.

Developmental. Refers to the progressive and continuous changes in a system; the result is growth, or movement from one developmental stage to another.

Dominance theory. The idea that some dogs want to be on top and will fight with their species and humans for top-dog positions.

Dysfunctional. Impaired functioning.

Enhance. To make greater, better, or more enchanting.

Environmental. In animal behavior consulting, refers to the role of environmental factors in the causation of behavior.

Extremists. Not moderate in their views and possibly militant; extremists advocate for and resort to measures beyond the norm.

Feedback. The return of information to the system; in behavior consulting, applies to cues from dogs and families that tell us how they are responding to other's movements; applies also to information from consultants to families.

Good-enough families. Meet the needs of members to adequately solve problems, and support good-enough functioning.

Militant. Having a combative character; aggressive in the service of a cause.

Narcissistic. Refers to a personality disorder characterized by a grandiose sense of self-importance, lack of
empathy, need for excessive admiration, sense of
entitlement; interpersonally exploitative; arrogant,
haughty; often envious of others or believes others are
envious of him.[2]

Operant. Refers to a dog's ability to control rein-
forcements through their own initiative. The dog can
make good things happen and because rewards follow,
he repeats behaviors that bring him what he wants.

Owner reinforcement. A term used to describe dog's
behaviors that are reinforced by owners. Families
often inadvertently reinforce undesirable behaviors in
dogs.

Scapegoat. Persons or animals who are blamed for
the actions of others, and perhaps receive punishment
for same.

Self-actualization. To develop or achieve one's fullest
potential; to be on the path to realizing one's possibilities.

Self-determination. Relates to the dynamic of free
will and having the freedom to determine one's own
course of action without coercion or compulsion.

---

[2] Diagnostic Criteria from DMS-IV. American Psychiatric Association.

References and Suggested Reading

Albert, A. and Bulcroft, K. (1988). *Pets, families, and the life course*. Journal of Marriage and Family Therapy, 50. p. 543-52

Aloff, Brenda. (2002) *Aggression in Dogs: Practical Management, Prevention & Behaviour Modification*. TFH Publications: New Jersey

Bailey, Jon and Mary Burch (2006) *How to Think Like a Behavior Analyst*. Lawrence Erlbaum Associates: New Jersey

Burch, Mary and Jon Bailey (1999). *How Dogs Learn*. Howell Book House: New York

Cain, A.O. (1983) A study of pets in the family system. In *New Perspectives on Our Lives with Companion Animals,* ed. A.H. Katcher and A.M. Beck. University of Pennsylvania Press: Philadelphia. p. 72-81

Erikson, Erik (1993) *Childhood and Society*. Norton, W. W. and Company, Inc.: New York

Gause, Donald and Gerald Weinberg (1992) *Are Your Lights On? How to Figure Out What the Problem Really Is.* Dorset House Publishing: New York

Guerin, Philip and Thomas Fogarty (1996) *Working with Relationship Triangles.* The Guilford Press: New York

Kerr, Michael, (1981) "Family Systems Theory and Therapy." Chapter 7, *Handbook of Family Therapy.* Edited by Alan S. Gurman, and David P. Kniskern, Brunner/Mazel: New York

Lindsay, Steven (2005) *Handbook of Applied Dog Behavior and Training, Volume Three: Procedures and Protocols.* Blackwell Publishing: Iowa

Lindsay, Steven (2001) *Applied Dog Behavior and Training, Volume Two: Etiology and Assessment of Behavior Problems.* Iowa State University Press: Ames

Metcalf, L., F.N. Thomas, S.D. Miller, and M.A. Hubble (1996). *What works in solution-focused brief therapy: A qualitative analysis of client and therapist perceptions.* In S.D. Miller, M.A. Hubble, and B.L. Duncan (Eds.), *Handbook of Solution-Focused Brief Therapy,* (pp. 335-349). Jossey-Bass: San Francisco

Milani, Myrna. (1995) *Art of Veterinary Practice: A Guide to Client Communications.* University of Pennsylvania Press

Minuchin, Salvador and H. Charles Fishman (2003) *Family Healing: Strategies for Hope and Understanding.* Simon and Schuster: New York.

Minuchin, Salvador and H. Charles Fishman (1990) *Family Therapy Techniques.* Harvard University Press: Cambridge

Nichols, M and R. Schwarz, R. (2003) *Bowen family systems therapy* in MP. Nichols and R.C. Schwartz, *Family Therapy: Concepts and Methods.* 5th ed., Allyn and Bacon: Boston

Odell, M., T.J. Butler, and M.B. Dielman (1997) *Client experiences of solution focused couple therapy.* Paper presented at the 55th Annual American Association for Marriage and Family Therapy Conference.

Overall, Karen (1993) *Clinical Behavioral Medicine for Small Animals.* Elsevier Health Services: Philadelphia

Parsons, Emma (2005) *Click to Calm: Healing the Aggressive Dog.* Sunshine Books: Waltham

Pierce, R. Counselor respect (1967. In R. R. Carkhuff (Ed.), *The counselor's contributions to facilitative processes.* Urbana, Ill.: Parkinson

Rokeach, Milton (2000) *Understanding Human Values: Individual and Societal.* Simon and Schuster: New York

Rokeach, Milton (1973) *The Nature of Human Values.* The Free Press: New York

Serpell, James (2003) *The Domestic Dog: its evolution, behaviour and interactions with people.* James Serpell, editor. Cambridge University Press: New York

Shyrock, Jen. (2005) *Dogs and Storks™ Educational CD Download.* Web: www.familypaws.com

Sommers-Flanagan, Rita, PhD and J. Sommers-Flanagan, PhD. (1999) *Clinical Interviewing.* John Wiley and Sons, Inc.: New York

Thomas, Lewis. (1995) *Lives of a Cell: Notes of a Biology Watcher.* Penguin Books: New York.

Wallerstein, Judith, Julia Lewis & Sandra Blakeslee. (2000) *The Unexpected Legacy of Divorce: A 25 Year Landmark Study.* Hyperion: New York

Weinberg, Dani (2006) *Teaching People Teaching Dogs.* Howln Moon Press: New York

INDEX

A

Ackerman, Dr. Nathan, 11
Adopt. *See* Rescue
Anxiety, 9, 48, 49, 50, 65, 66,
    99, 140, *See* Separation
    Anxiety
    electronic tools, 17
    in triangulation, 14, 46,
        47, 48, 54
Aragorn, 12
Arousal, 8, 9, 65, 93, 107
Aversives, 22, 77, 78, 98, *See*
    Training Tools

B

Bach, Chris, 26
Behavior consultant, 4, 36,
    37, 40, 43, 44, 45, 49, 50,
    54, 56, 64, 67, 70, 77, 80,
    83, 91, 101, 103-109, 121,
    125, 130, 134, 137-138,
    140-141
Behaviorist, 4, *See*
    Veterinary
    Skinnerian, 140

Biting, 13, 17, 18, 25, 29, 30,
    31, 38, 39, 44, 64, 69, 70,
    85, 88, 89, 94, 95, 104,
    114, 115, 117, 131, 132,
    133
Blaming, 41, 45, 51, 66, 85,
    87, 90, 107
Borderline personality
    disorder, 126
Boundaries, 13, 14, 59, 72,
    103, 111, 116
Bowen, Murray, 46, 48, 50,
    53, 126, 129

C

Carter, Dr. Elizabeth, 60
Change, 6, 13, 14, 15, 20, 22,
    50, 54, 55, 56, 59, 61, 63,
    65, 67, 68, 72, 74, 75, 80,
    83, 84, 88, 92, 102
Children, 7, 11, 14, 28, 29,
    34, 35, 38, 41, 42, 45, 52,
    57, 59, 60, 65, 66, 67, 68,
    69, 70, 71, 72, 73, 75, 81,
    110, 112, 117, 119
    adolescent, 36, 45, 49, 70,
        72, 73, 76, 114, 115

168

Clomicalm, 100
Coalition. *See* Triangles
Coercion, 143
Collaborative Healthcare,
    101
    IAABC statement, 153
Companionship, 14, 26, 36,
    42, 44, 56, 64, 70, 73, 130,
    140
Competence, 4, 42, 47, 49,
    52, 65, 66, 119, 129, 139,
    144
Competition, 16, 34
Containment, 17, 18, 85
Context, 7, 8, 9, 52
Contract, 6, 83, 101, 109, 133
Couple, 7, 15, 16-18, 35, 38,
    39, 40, 41, 52, 59, 60, 65,
    67, 76, 80, 81, 84, 85, 86,
    87, 91, 107, 108, 113, 114,
    137
Crate, 9, 29, 49, 96, 97, 98,
    99, 101, 107, 117

D

Daycare, 65
Developmental, 9, 13, 20, 55,
    56, 58, 63, 74, 95, 125, 134
Differentiation, 59, 61, 126,
    128, 129
Divorce, 23, 56, 64, 73, 74
Doberman, 81
Dominance, 14, 18, 21-22, 35,
    46, 102, 103-104
Dysfunction, 5, 31, 35, 46,
    51, 83, 103, 117, 142, 144

E

Elderly, 43, 60, 75, 80, 81, 88
Elimination, 29, 44, 45, 49,
    87, 131, 139

Emerson, Ralph Waldo, 121
Emotionality, 13, 15, 36, 42,
    43, 45, 48, 51, 53, 54, 59,
    61, 63, 68, 72, 75, 77, 122,
    125-126, 129, 140, 144
Empathy, 130, 131, 133, 134
Enactment, 105-106, 107
Euthanasia, 39, 46, 64, 70,
    85, 89, 115
Exaggeration, 144-145
Extremism, 114, 145

F

Family counselor, 6
Family of origin, 61-62, 63
Family system, 7, 21, 36, 46,
    48, 65, 83, 85, 126, 129,
    163
    individuals as, 7, 8, 11, 12,
    20, 24, 52, 63, 75, 109,
    127, 128-129, 136, 138,
    142
Family therapy, 11, 91
Family-of-origin, 52
Fears, phobias, 9, 17, 43, 50,
    69, 84, 86, 102, 103, 108,
    111, 113, 134, 140, 143,
    See Owner reinforcement
Fishman, Dr. H. Charles, 7

G

German Shepherd, 76, 78
Goals, 13, 16, 66, 78, 83, 93,
    94, 96, 105, 114, 116-118,
    142
Grandparenting, 5, 59, 68,
    72
Grief, loss, 15, 46, 140
Groomers, 5, 9, 28, 37, 54

H

Harp music, 96
Homeostasis, 83, 102, 119
Humility, 14, 57

I

Intensity, 113, 115, 116
International Association of
    Animal Behavior
    Consultants, 70, 153
    ethics, 70, 77

J

Joining, 1, 24, 25, 34, 35, 41,
    51, 53, 59, 63, 68, 89, 91,
    92, 93, 94, 95, 103, 104,
    109, 111, 124, 138

L

Labrador Retriever, 36, 70,
    107, 132
Leadership, 11, 36, 37, 43,
    44, 49, 69, 79, 90, 92, 103,
    106, 108, 110, 123, 129
Leash aggression, 15, 79
Lewis, C.S., 121
Lifecycle, 9, 55, 56, 57, 58,
    61, 63, 68, 72, 75, 80, 149
Loss, See grief, loss

M

Martin Luther King, 142
Maturity, 12, 92, 122, 125,
    126, 137
McGoldrick, Dr. Monica, 58,
    60

Medication, 39, 99, 100, 101,
    114
Mental illness, 66, 126
Minuchin, Dr. Salvador, 8,
    33, 91, 95, 102
Mortensen, Viggo, 12

N

Narcissism, 126
Negative campaigning, 142,
    144
Nonjudgmental, 104, 131

O

Over/under functioning, 117,
    118
Overall, Dr. Karen, 96

P

Positive regard, 19, 20, 92,
    112, 113, 121, 123, 124,
    128, 133, 135, 143
Problem solving, 5, 13, 20,
    24, 35, 37, 45, 47-49, 57,
    66, 81, 84, 88, 91, 93, 102-
    103, 109, 112, 118, 122,
    125
Protection, 13, 18, 25, 26, 29,
    30, 43, 44, 51, 62, 66-67,
    69, 73, 78, 81, 86-87, 89,
    92, 96, 102, 103, 104, 112,
    144
Puppy mill, 90

R

Raimond, Sue, 96
React/reactivity, 8, 25, 28,
    45, 48, 54, 85, 126, 141

Reframing, 22, 102, 103- 105
Rehoming, 18, 43, 67
Reinforcement, 9, 27, 29, 35,
    49, 69, 104, 108
Rejection, 21, 42, 49, 51, 98,
    126
Rescue, 13, 15, 18, 31, 27, 44,
    46, 51, 54, 62, 66, 85, 90,
    96, 113, 116, 133
Resource guarding, 15, 67
Right relationship, 13, 44, 96
Rokeach, Dr. Milton, 136
Roles, 11, 25-26, 37, 44, 46,
    53, 56, 59, 60, 64, 68, 75,
    80, 93, 116, 119, 144
Rules, 9, 11, 13, 17-18, 19,
    22-25, 26, 27, 28, 30-31,
    42, 45, 49, 74, 92, 94, 106,
    108, 114

S

Scapegoat, 35, 41, 51, 94, 162
Self, 11, 12, 13, 20, 25, 33,
    36, 41, 59, 61, 80, 126,
    127, 128, 135
    differentiation, 126, 127,
        128, 129
    pseudoself, 127
    self-awareness, 106, 122,
        125, 129, 130, 134, 136
    self-concept, 127
    self-contained, 8
    self-control, 36
    self-definition, 126
    self-determination, 11, 112
    self-respect, 137
    solid self, 127, 128
    use of, 130
Separation Anxiety, 95, 96,
    99, 100, 114, 122
Shelter. *See* Rescue
Social change, 142, *See*
    coercion, *See* negative

campaigning, *See*
    exaggeration
Activism, 128, 142
Symptom, 65, 85
    medical, 65
    sympton bearers, 7
Systems theory, 7, 46, 126

T

The Third Way
    Chris Bach, 127
Tolkien, 11
Toy dogs, 13, 43, 44
    Maltese, 70
    Yorkie, 105, 117
    Yorkshire, 73
Triangles
    flexible, 35
Training
    alpha rolls, 144
Training tools, 27, 34, 50,
    108, 110, *See* Containment
    choke collars, 27, 77, 78,
        110
    confinement, 107
    harness, Premier Easy
        Walk, 78
    electronic, 17, 18, 27, 85
    prong collar, 27
    relaxation, 96
    techniques, 78
Triangles, 9, 33, 35, 37, 38,
    40, 43, 45, 46, 47, 48, 54
Triangulation.. *See* cherry-
    picking, *See* triangles

V

Values, 8, 11, 19, 20, 21, 23,
    26, 63, 64-65, 74, 90-91,
    110, 112, 117, 124, 134,
    135,-136, 151

Veterinarian, 38, 39, 64, 99,
100, 101

Veterinary behaviorist, 100